PACKAGE DESIGN IN JAPAN

© Benedikt Taschen Verlag GmbH & Co. KG,
Balthasarstraße 79, D-5000 Köln, 1989
© Rikuyo-sha Publishing, Inc., 1988
Shigeru Uchida
Redaktion und Produktion: Fricke GmbH, Frankfurt
Satz: Dhyana Fotosatz, Frankfurt
Gesamtherstellung: Druckerei Ernst Uhl, Radolfzell
Umschlaggestaltung: Detlev Schaper, Köln
Printed in West Germany
ISBN 3-8228-0393-6

PACKAGE DESIGN
IN JAPAN

TASCHEN

CONTENTS

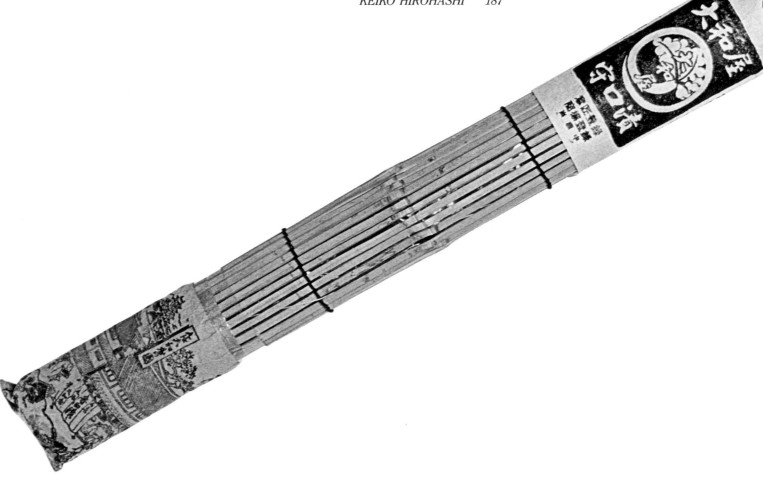

fruits
Früchte
fruits

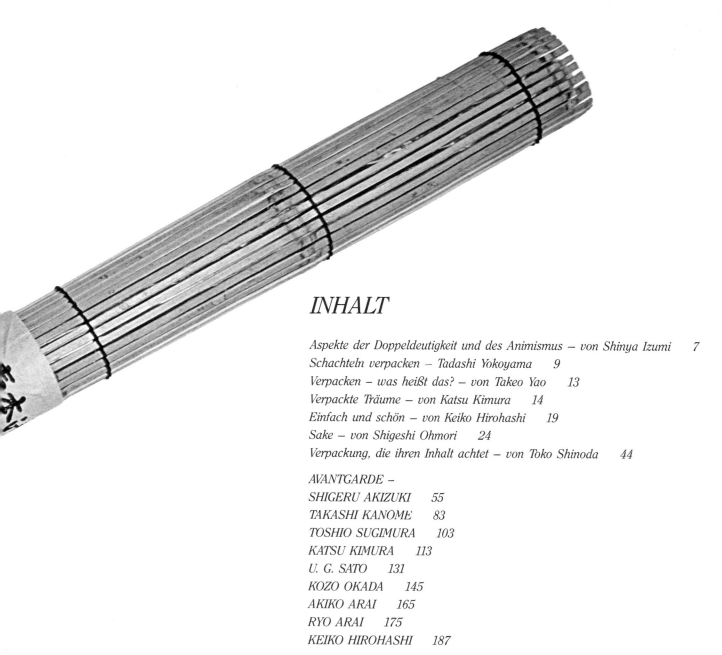

INHALT

SOMMAIRE

lunch box
Lunchbox
boîte pique-nique

ASPECTS OF AMBIGUITY AND ANIMISM
ASPEKTE DER DOPPELDEUTIGKEIT UND DES ANIMISMUS
DES ASPECTS D'AMBIGUITÉ ET D'ANIMISME

Japanese package design has a number of unique characteristics. The first of these unique characteristics is the coexistence of traditional and modern design elements. Of course, the same elements are in evidence in all the other nations of the world as well. However, there is probably not any other country where the existence of both is found on such a large scale or where they are both so vigorously supported by the general public as in Japan.

The traditional aspect has two faces. One is the physical tradition. For instance, the Japanese are particularly skilled at bringing out the unique qualities of natural materials. And this is evident in the field of package design too. There are numerous practical examples that could be mentioned, such as baskets made of straw, dishes made of clam shells, and packaging from the leaves of the cherry tree or bamboo grass. In the case of bamboo grass, its sterilization properties have been recognized and utilized for the purpose of preservation. Also the light wood of the paulownia tree with its superior moisture proofing, its insecticide, and its fireproofing qualities has been used to create a large number of fine packages. These traditional methods are still very much in use today.

"Lightness" and "rigidity" are often presented as distinctive features of Japanese culture. But these comprise only one aspect of the design of Japan which also possesses the seemingly contradictory attributes of "simplicity" and "splendour".

Along with works that utilize traditional Japanese design elements, there are also numerous items which incorporate such Westernised designs that they appear to have been imported directly from Europe or America.

The second major characteristic is bound up with the fact that Japanese culture belongs to the world of polytheism, and specifically to the cultural classification of animism. Since the ancient past, the Japanese have believed in eight million gods and recognize their presence in all material objects. We even believe that there is a deity in each drinking glass and chair. But these deities are not the God of the West. Nor are they the Idea of Greek philosophy. Rather they are far closer to such concepts as Anima or Nature.

Japanisches Verpackungsdesign weist eine Vielzahl einzigartiger Merkmale auf. Die erste Besonderheit ist das Zusammenwirken von traditionellen und modernen Designelementen. Natürlich treten diese Elemente auch in anderen Ländern als Japan in Erscheinung. Doch es gibt wohl kaum ein anderes Land, in dem beide Sphären sich in so großem Maße manifestieren, wo beide Sphären von der Allgemeinheit so selbstverständlich gestützt werden wie in Japan.

Der traditionelle Aspekt hat zwei Gesichter. Das eine entspricht der physischen Tradition. So verstehen es die Japaner besonders, die Eigenschaft natürlicher Materialien zur Geltung zu bringen. Und dies zeigt sich eben auch auf dem Gebiet des Verpackungsdesigns. Viele Beispiele könnten hier angeführt werden, etwa aus Reisstroh geflochtene Körbe, Schalen oder Eßplättchen aus Muscheln, Hüllen aus Kirschzweigen, Blättern oder Bambusgras. Nachdem man die sterilisierenden Eigenschaften des Bambus erkannt hat, benutzt man dieses Material auch für die Konservierung. Auch das leichte Holz der *Paulownie* mit seinen feuerfesten, insektenabschreckenden, feuchtigkeitsbewahrenden Eigenschaften ist ein hervorragendes Material, um die verschiedensten Verpackungen und Umhüllungen herzustellen. Die überlieferten Verfahren sind noch heute überall gebräuchlich.

„Leichtigkeit" und gleichzeitig „Strenge" werden oft als spezifische Merkmale der japanischen Kultur hervorgehoben. Doch das ist nur eine Sicht der Kultur Japans; sie umschließt darüber hinaus so gegensätzliche Eigenschaften wie Einfachheit einerseits und Prachtentfaltung andererseits. Sie alle finden Ausdruck auch in der Farbe als Träger vielfältiger Symbolbedeutungen.

Neben Arbeiten, die traditionelle japanische Design-Elemente aufnehmen, gibt es Entwürfe mit so ausgeprägt „westlichem" Design, als ob sie direkt aus Europa oder Amerika importiert worden wären.

Das zweite Charakteristikum japanischer Verpackung hängt mit der japanischen Besonderheit des Animismus (der Allbelebtheit) zusammen. Seit Urzeiten glauben die Japaner an Millionen von Göttern und erkennen deren Anwesenheit in jedem sichtbaren Gegenstand, selbst in einem Trinkglas oder einem Möbelstück. All diese Gottheiten fin-

Le design d'emballage japonais est marqué par plusieurs particularités. La première en est la coexistence d'éléments de conception traditionnels et modernes. Bien sûr, les mêmes éléments apparaissent dans toutes les nations du monde. Cependant, il n'existe probablement aucun pays où l'existence de ces deux catégories peut être ressentie à un tel niveau et où toutes deux sont si vigoureusement soutenues par le grand public qu'au Japon.

L'aspect traditionnel a deux visages. L'un correspond à la tradition physique. Ainsi, par exemple, les Japonais sont particulièrement habiles pour mettre en valeur les qualités des matières naturelles. Et ceci se manifeste également dans le domaine du design d'emballage. De nombreux exemples pourraient être énumérés à cet endroit, tels que des paniers faits à base de paille, des objets usuels produits à base de coquillages, ou des paquets fabriqués à l'aide de feuilles de cerisiers ou de bambou. En ce qui concerne le bambou, on l'utilise aussi dans le domaine de la conservation depuis que l'on a reconnu ses qualités de stérilité. Le bois léger de l'arbre paulownia a lui aussi permis la création d'un grand nombre de jolis emballages grâce à sa nature ignifuge et hydrofuge ainsi que ses qualités d'insecticide. Ces méthodes traditionnelles sont encore en usage aujourd'hui.

«Douceur» et «rigueur» ont souvent été soulignées comme traits caractéristiques de la culture japonaise. Mais ceci n'est que partiellement correct, car notre culture possède également les attributs opposés de «simplicité vigoureuse» et «splendeur».

Mis à part certaines œuvres dans lesquelles ces éléments traditionnels du design japonais ont été thématisés, on trouve aussi de nombreux exemples tenus dans un design tellement «occidentalisé» qu'on a l'impression qu'ils ont été directement importés d'Europe où d'Amérique.

La deuxième particularité majeure provient du fait que la culture japonaise fait partie de l'univers du polythéisme, notamment de la classification culturelle de l'animisme. Depuis l'antiquité, les Japonais croient en huit millions de dieux dont ils discernent la présence dans chaque objet. Nous croyons même qu'il existe une déité dans chaque verre ou dans chaque chaise. Mais ces déités ne correspondent point au Dieu des civilisations occidentales. Et pas non plus à l'Idée de la philosophie grecque.

In any case, to the Japanese any physical object is more than simple matter as it contains the presence of some "being". Thus for the Japanese, packaging is not made merely to cover a piece of physical matter, but is meant to house the "being" present there as well. This depth psychology of the Japanese results in the anthropomorphism of all objects and gives rise to ideas such as that things are attempting to escape from the constraints of their packaging and so forth.

The presence of both the traditional and modern aspects in the work of a single designer is one of the unique characteristics of Japanese designers. Thus the same designer sometimes creates designs that are extremely traditional and at other times produces highly modern, Western style designs. No Japanese designer, however, feels the slightest sense of contradiction in this phenomenon.

Shinya Izumi

den in dem Einen Gott der westlichen Religionen keine Entspechung, auch nicht in der Auffassung der griechischen Philosophie. Dagegen kommen sie solchen Begriffen wie *Seele* oder *Natur* schon sehr nahe.

Jedenfalls ist jeder materielle Gegenstand für die Japaner mehr als nur einfache Substanz, da es die Gegenwart irgendwelchen *Lebens* in sich birgt. Somit dient die Verpackungskunst nicht allein dazu, einen materiellen Gegenstand einzuhüllen, sondern sie *bedeutet* auch, dem mit „Leben" erfüllten Geschenk eine Behausung zu geben. Diese besondere japanische Einfühlsamkeit führt zu einem antropomorphen Verständnis aller Dinge und bringt Gedanken hervor wie den, daß Gegenstände immer wieder versuchen, aus der Enge ihrer Umhüllung auszubrechen . . .

Das Vorhandensein dieser beiden Aspekte, von Tradition und Moderne im Werk eines einzelnen Designers, ist eine der Besonderheiten japanischen Designs. So entwirft ein und derselbe Künstler ein Design, das extrem traditionell ist, und bei nächster Gelegenheit ein ausgesprochen – westlich – modernes. Und keiner sieht darin auch nur den geringsten Widerspruch.

Shinya Izumi

Par contre, ils ressemblent bien plus à des concepts tels que «l'âme» où «la nature».

Pour les Japonais, chaque objet physique est bien plus qu'une simple matière puisqu'il contient la présence d'une «existence». Ainsi, pour les Japonais, non seulement la création d'un emballage sert à envelopper un objet matériel, mais elle signifie aussi donner un abri au cadeau rempli de vie. Cette profondeur japonaise particulière amène à la conclusion que tous les objet tentent sans relâche de s'echapper de leur enveloppe trop étrolte . . .

La présence d'éléments traditionnels et modernes dans l'œuvre du même designer est une des particularités des designers japonais. Ainsi, le même designer crée parfois des œuvres de style extrêment traditionnel alors qu'il produit d'autres fois des œuvres modernes de style «occidental». Et personne n'y voit le moindre soupçon de contradiction.

Shinya Izumi

WRAPPING AND BOXES
SCHACHTELN VERPACKEN
DES BOÎTES ET LEUR EMBALLAGE

Whenever you buy something at a Japanese department store it is wrapped up for you in attractive paper that has been created by a designer. Nowadays simple bags are often used to wrap small items; however, on request you can get even a single notebook wrapped with the greatest of care. And any shop you go to in any town will be sure to have its own specially designed wrapping paper, and some of them are so very attractive that after you unwrap the package you feel a pang of regret at throwing the wrapping paper away. This custom is the exact opposite of common practice in most shops in Europe and America where you normally come out of the store with your merchandise thrown carelessly into a plain, nondescript paper bag.

When you stop to consider why this difference exists, you come to the conclusion that it is probably because the act of wrapping things has always held a special significance for the Japanese. While the major element involved is indeed what is inside, the Japanese believe that the feelings of respect or gratitude of either the presenter or the seller of a package are revealed in the way in which he has wrapped it. Apart from actual wrapping paper, the Japanese have various methods for wrapping things, including the special celebratory wrapper called *noshigami,* the small crêpe wrapper called a *fukusa,* and the cloth wrapper that comes in a wide variety of sizes known as a *furoshiki.*

So parents teach their children how to wrap things properly, and everyone is so sensitive to the way things that they receive are wrapped that if something is wrapped carelessly, they feel that the giver's intentions are not quite what they should be. Thus the Japanese often take almost as much care in deciding how a certain item should be wrapped for a certain occasion as they do in selecting the gift itself. Perhaps this tradition is the reason one sees so very many package designs in present-day Japan that possess a wrapping image, particularly when compared to their counterparts in Europe or America. Kanome's wrapping paper for Okoshi uses an altered form of the *noshigami* wrapper in its design, and in Kimura's wrapping paper design for Yokan and Kanome's box design for Mizu-Yokan, we see references to the popular designs found in the *fukusa* and the *furoshiki* respectively.

Wenn Sie in einem japanischen Kaufhaus etwas einkaufen, wird es für Sie in hübsches Papier, das von einem Designer entworfen wurde, eingeschlagen. Inzwischen ist man dazu übergegangen, für kleinere Gegenstände schlichte Tüten und Beutel zu verwenden, doch wenn Sie ausdrücklich darum bitten, wird Ihnen sogar ein einzelnes Notizbuch mit der größten Sorgfalt eingepackt. Und jedes beliebige Geschäft in jeder beliebigen Stadt wird es sich nicht nehmen lassen, ein selbst entworfenes Verpackungspapier zu führen. Es ist manchmal so schön, daß man nach dem Auspacken der Ware Gewissensbisse bekommt, es einfach wegzuwerfen. Diese Gepflogenheit ist das Gegenteil von dem, was man in europäischen oder amerikanischen Läden erlebt; dort wird die eingekaufte Ware unachtsam in eine unförmige Papiertüte gestopft.

Wenn Sie kurz innehalten und überlegen, wieso dieser Unterschied besteht, werden Sie zu dem Schluß kommen, daß es wahrscheinlich daran liegt, daß der Vorgang des Einpackens schon seit jeher eine besondere Bedeutung für die Japaner gehabt hat. Während außerhalb Japans das Wesentliche der Sache die Frage ist, was sich im Inneren einer Schachtel befindet, glauben die Japaner, daß sich die Empfindungen von Respekt oder von Dankbarkeit des Schenkenden sowohl wie des Verkaufenden in der Art und Weise offenbaren, wie er die Geschenkbox verpackt hat. Vom Einwickelpapier abgesehen kennen die Japaner die unterschiedlichsten Verfahren, etwas einzupacken, einschließlich *nashigami, fukusa* und *furoshiki* in den unterschiedlichsten Formaten.

So bringen Eltern ihren Kindern bei, wie man die Dinge richtig einpackt, und jeder achtet so sehr darauf, wie die Geschenke, die er erhält, eingepackt sind, daß er sich von den Absichten des Schenkenden betrogen fühlt, wenn ein Präsent lieblos eingepackt ist. Folglich geben sich die Japaner bei der Entscheidung, wie ein bestimmter Gegenstand für einen bestimmten Anlaß eingepackt werden soll, oft ebensoviel Mühe wie bei der Auswahl des Geschenks selbst.

Vielleicht ist diese Gepflogenheit der Grund dafür, warum man im heutigen Japan so vielen Warenpackungen begegnet, die so gestaltet sind, als seien es Geschenkpackungen, vor allem im Vergleich mit ihren Pendants in Europa und Amerika.

Quand vous achetez quelque chose dans un grand magasin japonais, on empaquette votre achat dans un ravissant papier créé par un designer. De nos jours, on tend à utiliser des sacs et des sachets sobres pour les petits objets, mais si vous le demandez expressément, on vous emballera même un simple carnet avec le plus grand soin. N'importe quel magasin dans n'importe quelle ville tient son propre papier d'emballage créé spécialement pour la maison. Ceux-ci sont parfois tellement ravissants que l'on éprouve des remords à jeter l'emballage une fois que l'on a dépaqueté son achat. Cette coutume est le contraire de ce qui arrive dans la plupart des cas à quelqu'un qui sort d'un magasin en Europe ou en Amérique – ses achats ont été bourrés sans aucun soin dans un sac de papier informe.

Quand vous vous demandez pourquoi cette différence existe, vous en venez à la conclusion que c'est probablement parce que l'acte d'emballer des objets a depuis toujours une importance très spéciale pour les Japonais. Alors que pour nous l'essentiel est en fait ce qui se trouve à l'intérieur d'un emballage, les Japonais, eux, croient que les sentiments de respect ou de gratitude soit de son donateur, soit de son vendeur, se révèlent dans la façon dont il a empaqueté l'objet en question. Mis à part le matériel d'emballage proprement dit, les Japonais connaissent diverses méthodes pour empaqueter des objets, y compris le *noshigami,* le *fukusa* et le *furoshiki.*

Ainsi, les parents apprennent à leurs enfants comment on emballe des objets correctement et chacun fait tellement attention à la façon dont les cadeaux qu'il reçoit sont empaquetés que quand un présent n'est point empaqueté avec beaucoup de soin, qu'il se sent trahi par les intentions de son donateur. Ainsi, les Japonais apportent pratiquement le même soin à décider comment empaqueter un certain objet pour une occasion précise qu'au choix du cadeau lui-même.

Cette tradition est peut-être bien la raison pour laquelle on trouve de nos jours au Japon tant d'emballages de marchandises stylés comme s'il s'agissait d'emballages-cadeaux, surtout si l'on compare ce fait avec la situation opposée observée en Europe ou en Amérique. Kanome modifie dans son design de papier d'emballage pour la vieille compa-

Akizuki's neat bag with the silver background covered with blue pine needles is also reminiscent of a stylish *furoshiki* pattern. Hirohashi's stationery series patterns also remind us of the designs found on traditional *chiyogami* and *furoshiki,* and the diagonal lines found here are clearly taken from the wrapping traditions of Japan rather than those of Europe. Since things to be wrapped in a *fukusa* or a *furoshiki* are placed on the wrapper on the diagonal, diagonal lines naturally appear in the package when the item has been wrapped.

Of course, the pleasure of wrapping does not come only in the still life effect of the appearance of the finished package. Everybody has experienced the thrill of curiosity and expectation concerning the contents as a beautiful package is carefully unwrapped.

It is no exaggeration to say that wrappings were made primarily for this sense of pure enjoyment. When a package is opened, it is usual that the inside of the wrapping paper is seen. The traditions of Japan have never forgotten this moment of anticipation. Unexpected brilliant colors and varied patterns that appear during the process of unwrapping a package have always been a part of our aesthetic experience. This consideration is in evidence in Hirohashi's stationery series, and it has been utilized particularly effectively in all the works by Akizuki. He received his inspiration from the construction of the traditional folding box. The brilliant inside surfaces concealed behind the all black outer surfaces of Kimura's gift boxes are almost an illustrated explanation of this same aesthetic mechanism.

But today's packaging design, as a part of commercial design, has been burdened with the mission of showing off the contents to make them attractive and enticing to the prospective customer. No matter how beautifully or cleverly a package has been devised, it is merely an image advertisement for what is inside, or a contents signboard. It only serves its purpose if it proves effective as a communication mechanism. Most of these wrappers are fated to be tossed into the waste-paper basket as soon as the pleasure of unwrapping has been savored.

On the other hand, some packages should have expectations of a second life after their primary

Kanome variiert bei seinem Packpapier für das altehrwürdige Handelshaus Okoshi das *noshigami;* und in Kimuras Einwickelpapier für Yokan-Konfekt sowie in Kanomes Entwurf für die Yokan-Konfektschachtel sind Bezüge zu den altbekannten Mustern von *fukusa* und *furoshiki* zu finden. Auch Akizukis hübsche Tragetasche mit den blauen Piniennadeln auf silberfarbenem Untergrund erinnert an das stilisierte *furoshiki*-Dekor. Ebenso erinnern Hiroshashis Muster für Standardserien an traditionelle Entwürfe, und die Diagonalen hier stammen zweifellos eher aus der japanischen als aus Europas Verpackungstradition (*fukusa* oder *furoshiki* verlangen, daß der zu verpackende Gegenstand diagonal auf die Unterlage gelegt wird). Natürlich endet das Vergnügen am Einpacken nicht bei der Betrachtung eines Stillebens. Jeder kennt den Nervenkitzel, den Erwartung und Neugier auf den Inhalt der Verpackung hervorrufen, wenn ein schön verpacktes Geschenk behutsam aufgemacht wird.

Angesichts dieses Glücksgefühls kann man wohl sagen, daß Verpackungen vor allem für diesen Augenblick des Auspackens gemacht werden. Wenn eine Verpackung geöffnet wird, dann erblickt man als erstes die Innenseite des Verpackungsmaterials. In der japanischen Tradition hat man diese Vorfreude nie vergessen.

Unerwartete, leuchtende Farben und unterschiedliche Muster, die während des Auspackens sichtbar werden, sind seit jeher ein Bestandteil unseres ästhetischen Empfindens gewesen. Das wird sichtbar in Hiroshashis Standardserien und nirgendwo deutlicher als in allen Arbeiten von Akizuki. Ihm diente die Konstruktion der traditionellen Faltschachtel als Anregung. Auch die schimmernden Innenflächen hinter den tiefschwarzen Außenflächen der Geschenkboxen stellen fast eine bildliche Erläuterung eben dieses ästhetischen Vorgangs dar.

Doch dem heutigen Verpackungsdesign als Teil des Warenkonzepts obliegt es, den Packungs*inhalt* vorteilhaft zur Geltung zu bringen, um ihn damit für den potentiellen Käufer attraktiver und verlockend zu machen. Da spielt es keine Rolle mehr, wie schön oder wie intelligent eine Verpackung konzipiert worden ist, sie ist nur mehr ein Verkaufssignal für den Inhalt. Sie hat nur dann ihren Zweck er-

gnie de commerce Okoshi le *noshigami*, et le dessin de papier d'emballage de Kimura pour Yokan ainsi que le dessin de boîte de Kanome pour Mizu-Yokan présentent des références au design populaire que l'on trouve notamment dans le *fukusa* et le *furoshiki*. De même, le gentil sac d'Akizuki avec des aiguilles de pin bleues sur un fond argenté nous rappelle un dessin *furoshiki* stylisé. Les dessins de Hirohashi pour des produits de série nous font également penser aux prototypes que l'on trouve sur des *chiyogami* ou des *furoshiki* traditionnels; les lignes diagonales qu'on rencontre ici puisent leur origine plutôt dans les traditions de l'emballage du Japon que dans celles de l'Europe. Les objets destinés à être empaquetés dans un *fukusa* ou un *furoshiki* y sont posés en diagonale, les lignes diagonales apparaissent naturellement une fois le paquet terminé.

Cependant, le plaisir que l'on éprouve vis-à-vis d'un emballage ne provient pas exclusivement de l'effet de nature morte que nous offre un emballage achevé. Tout le monde connaît le frisson que causent la curiosité et l'espérance envers le contenu d'un paquet-cadeau lorsqu'on en défait son bel emballage. Quand on pense précisément à ce sentiment de bonheur, il ne semble pas exagéré de dire qu'un emballage est fait avant tout pour ce moment d'activité. Quand on ouvre un emballage, le regard tombe d'abord sur le côté intérieur du papier d'emballage. Le Japon n'a jamais oublié dans ses traditions ce moment de joie. Les couleurs vives inattendues et les multiples figures qui apparaissent au fur et à mesure qu'on défait un emballage ont depuis toujours fait partie de notre notion esthétique. Cette façon de penser est mise en évidence dans les séries standard de Hirohashi et n'a nulle part été plus profondément thématisée que dans l'œuvre d'Akizuki. Son inspiration est née de la construction d'une boîte pliante tradionnelle. Les surfaces intérieures brillantes cachées derrière des surfaces extérieures entièrement tenues en noir des boîtes-cadeaux Kimura peuvent également servir d'illustration du même mécanisme esthétique.

Mais on a imposé au design d'emballage d'aujourd'hui – qui fait partie du design commercial – le devoir de mettre en valeur son contenu afin de le rendre attractif et attirant pour l'acheteur éven-

purpose has been achieved. For instance, there may well be a very large number of men who use the plain wooden cigar boxes with labels from strange and far-away countries as secret treasure chests for their own most precious things. I also know quite a number of women who use gift boxes covered with Kimura's designed paper as containers for their own secret treasures. Such boxes seem far more like a familiar friend with whom one can relax.

At this point you may assert that any package at all could serve this sort of purpose, but in practice this does not seem to be the case. It is rather difficult to explain the psychological mechanism involved here, but perhaps it can be explained in the following manner. A certain independence is demanded of the design of such boxes in order to give them a life of their own after they have served the commercial design purposes related above and their original contents have been removed.

Tadashi Yokoyama

füllt, wenn sie sich als wirksam in den kommunikativen Mechanismen erweist. Es ist das Schicksal der meisten Verpackungen, in den Papierkorb zu wandern, sobald das mit dem Auspacken verbundene Vergnügen ausgekostet ist.

Andererseits sollten manche Verpackungen nach Erfüllung ihrer eigentlichen Funktion Aussicht auf Wiederverwendung haben. Es mag zum Beispiel viele Männer geben, die die gewöhnlichen Zigarrenkistchen aus Holz mit den Labels aus fernen Ländern als heimliche Schatztruhen für ihre kostbarsten Sachen verwenden. Ich kenne auch eine ganze Reihe Frauen, die Geschenkkartons, mit Kimuras Geschenkpapier überzogen, als Behältnisse für ihre bestgehüteten Geheimnisse verwenden. Solche Schachteln sind wie ein vertrauter Freund, bei dem man sich entspannen kann.

An dieser Stelle werden Sie womöglich einwerfen, daß jede Verpackung solchen Zwecken dienen kann – doch scheint dies in der Praxis nicht der Fall zu sein. Es ist ziemlich schwierig, den psychologischen Vorgang zu erklären, der hier wirksam wird, doch ich möchte es folgendermaßen versuchen: Das Design solcher Schachteln erfordert eine gewisse Eigenständigkeit, sie muß Bestand haben, wenn der ursprüngliche Zweck erfüllt und der Inhalt entnommen ist.

Tadashi Yokoyama

tuel. Ainsi, il n'importe plus qu'un emballage soit beau et ait été conçu avec ingéniosité, il ne constitue plus qu'une image de réclame ou une enseigne pour son contenu. Il ne produit son effet que s'il se révèle efficace comme mécanisme de communication. Le sort de la plupart des emballages de cette catégorie est d'être jetés dans une corbeille à papier dès que le plaisir de les défaire a été savouré.

D'autre part, une partie des emballages devraient connaître un avenir qui leur garantit une réutilisation après que leur raison d'être primordiale a disparu. Ainsi, il est bien possible qu'une quantité d'hommes utilisent ces boîtes à cigares ordinaires recouvertes d'inscriptions provenant de pays exotiques comme écrin pour leurs trésors secrets. Je connais également un certain nombre de femmes qui se servent des boîtes-cadeaux recouvertes de papier dessiné par Kimura pour y garder leurs affaires les plus intimes.

Maintenant vous allez objecter que tout emballage peut revêtir ce genre de fonction – mais ce n'est pas le cas dans la pratique. Il est assez difficile d'expliquer le mécanisme psychologique déclenché ici, mais je veux néanmoins essayer de le faire de la manière suivante. Le dessin de telles boîtes doit manifester une certaine indépendance capable de leur faire «mener une vie autonome» après que leur contenu d'origine en a été retiré et qu'il a rempli les fonctions commerciales mentionnées ci-dessus.

Tadashi Yokoyama

WHAT IS PACKAGING
VERPACKEN – WAS HEISST DAS
L'EMBALLAGE – QU'EST-CE QUE C'EST

The whole subject of package design has undergone a considerable change in recent years. More emphasis has been placed upon its function as a source of information to be conveyed to the consumer. We designers consider packaging as an important tool of communicaton.

Since the oil shock there has been public concern for saving natural resources, and various problems relating to the increased cost of packaging and the operation of disposal and safety have been discussed. Considering the future development of packaging, we must bear in mind the fact that packaging exists not for its own sake, but in order to satisfy consumer demand. By the time the packed article reaches the consumer it has passed through many hands, a process which must now be developed and simplified, especially in view of its close link to the question of cost.

We designers have been forced to learn many things in recent years. What was once considered to be good packaging suddenly became poor design. New printing processes and the discovery of new materials, while preserving our natural resources, have come to the fore. As a manufacturer, my desire is for the momentum of this current movement to spill over to package design. As establishing individual identity is becoming more and more important, today's package design must fit the individuality of each respective person. The package design which fails to meet this challenge will not survive in the future.

Takeo Yao

Das Verpackungsdesign hat in den letzten Jahren einen beachtlichen Wandel erlebt. Es wird mehr Wert auf seine informative Funktion gelegt, damit die Ware dem Verbraucher alle für ihn wichtigen Angaben signalisiert. Wir Designer betrachten die Verpackung als Mitte zur Kommunikation mit dem Verbraucher.

Nach der Ölkrise ist die Einsparung natürlicher Ressourcen zum öffentlichen Anliegen geworden, und viele Probleme im Zusammenhang mit gestiegenen Kosten, mit Entsorgung und Sicherheit, werden diskutiert. Was die zukünftige Entwicklung der Verpackung angeht, müssen wir wieder mehr dahin kommen, daß Verpackungen nicht so sehr Selbstzweck sind, sondern sich dem Verbraucher unterordnen, dem Menschen dienlich sind. Da die Waren beim Verpacken viele Hände und viele Arbeitsgänge durchlaufen, bevor sie den Verbraucher erreichen, muß eine Fortentwicklung im Sinne einer Vereinfachung des Verpackungsvorgangs erreicht werden. Dieses Problem hängt eng mit der Frage nach den Kosten zusammen.

Wir Designer haben in den letzten Jahren viel hinzulernen müssen. Was früher als gute Verpackung gegolten hatte, konnte plötzlich nicht mehr als gelungenes Design angesehen werden. Das Fortschreiten der Drucktechnik, die Entdeckung neuer schöner Werkstoffe im Zuge der Rohstoffeinsparung sind in den Vordergrund gerückt. Als Hersteller ist es mein Wunsch, daß der Segen dieses Fließens und Strömens der Zeit zurückstrahlt auf das Verpackungsdesign. Da sich heute die Individualität des Menschen allmählich wieder behauptet, wird es darauf ankommen, wie die Verpackungen der Individualität einer Person entsprechen werden. Verpackungsdesign, das auf diese Frage keine Antwort findet, wird in Zukunft nicht überleben können.

Takeo Yao

Les circonstances déterminant le design d'emballage ont connu un changement considérable pendant les dernières années. On a accordé plus d'importance à sa fonction informative, et c'était le devoir des marchandises de servir de médiateur des informations destinées aux consommateurs. Nous, les designers, considérons que l'emballage d'un article est un instrument important pour communiquer avec le consommateur.

Après la crise du pétrole, l'opinion publique a rémoigné beaucoup d'intérêt pour l'économie des ressources naturelles, et de nombreux problèmes concernant la détermination des coûts, notamment la hausse des frais d'emballage ou les questions d'élimination des déchers ainsi que de sécurité, ont été discutés. En ce qui concerne l'avenir de l'emballage, il nous revient de confirmer de nouveau qu'un emballage perçoit sa raison d'être des hommes et non des marchandises. Comme les marchandises passent par beaucoup de mains et beaucoup de procédés différents avant d'être remises aux consommateurs, il fallait améliorer l'emballage – à présent, il ne nous reste plus qu'à le simplifier. Il va falloir étudier ce sujet plus profondément que nous ne l'avons fait jusqu'à présent étant donné qu'il reste étroitement lié à la question des coûts. Nous, les designers, avons été forcés d'apprendre beaucoup de choses, ces dernières années. Un emballage considéré considéré comme bon dans le passé ne peut plus passer pour un bon design. Un nouveau procédé d'imprimerie, la découverte de la beauté de nouvelles matières permettant d'économiser des ressources naturelles, etc., sont passés au premier plan. En tant que producteur, mon désir est que la bénédiction de ce temps en dérive se réfléchisse sur le design d'emballage. Comme aujourd'hui l'identité de l'individu gagne de plus en plus d'importance, il devient nécessaire d'étudier à quel point les emballages sont capables de s'adapter à l'individualité des consommateurs. Un design d'emballage qui ne réussit pas à répondre à ce problème ne pourra désormais plus survivre.

Takeo Yao

noodles
Nudeln
pâtes

PACKAGING DREAMS
VERPACKTE TRÄUME
EMPAQUETER DES RÊVES

I became fond of sweets before I knew what was happening, though I also like *sake* – unfortunately a sure sign of diabetes. I like confectionery too. Confectionery within arm's reach – that's my dream.

Presumably to suit the convenience of trade, packages for expensive confectionery are comparatively few in number, and packages for everyday confectionery, such as *Yokan* (sweetened paste of beans), *Hi-gashi* (raw) and *Mochi-gashi* (rice cakes), which keep for days, are large in number. Elegant packages of *Kyo-gashi* (confectionery made in Kyoto) are especially beautiful. The unsophisticatedness of the Kanto district (where Tokyo is) is reflected in the originality of the *Edo-gashi* (confectionery from Tokyo) packaging which differs greatly from that of *Kyo-gashi*. Taking *Yokan* as an example, it is interesting that chip boxes were used in Edo to contain *Yokan*, and they, as the counterpart of the bamboo sheaths of Kyoto, express the characteristics of Edo.

Each district produces its own characteristic packages. Nagasaki and its confectionery in glass boxes at *sekku* are inseparably connected. Pretty bottles of confectionery in the shape of a fish or a wave, which I found at the storefront of Iwanaga-baiju-ken at Suwa-machi, used to be sold everywhere in Nagasaki though only two variations of them are seen today.

I wonder whether packaging design is developing.

Katsu Kimura

Ehe ich mich versah, bin ich ein Freund von Süßigkeiten geworden – und das, obwohl ich gleichzeitig ein Freund von *Sake* bin. Überflüssig zu sagen, daß dies ein Anzeichen von Diabetes ist. Darüberhinaus mag ich auch Konfekt. Konfekt in meiner Reichweite bringt mich zum Träumen.

Voller Träume, wie das Konfekt, muß natürlich auch seine Verpackung sein.

Relativ selten sind luxuriöse Verpackungen für teures Konfekt, wohl aus rein verkaufspraktischen Gründen. Es überwiegen eben die Verpackungen für die gängigen Näschereien: für *Yokan*-Konfekt (eine süße Bohnenpaste), für *Higashi*-Konfekt (halbroh) und *Mochigashi*-Reiskuchen, die sich länger halten.

Elegant sind die Verpackungen für *Kyo-gashi*, ein Konfekt, das in Kyoto hergestellt wird. Beim *Edo-gashi*-Konfekt, das in Tokio hergestellt wird, äußert sich die Eigenständigkeit des Kanto-Distrikts (in dem Tokio liegt) in einer Verpackung, die sich von der des *Kyo-gashi* sehr unterscheidet. Das *Yokan*-Konfekt zum Beispiel hat man in Tokio früher in Spanschachteln gefüllt – ein Gegenstück zu dem Bambusfutteral von Kyoto.

Jede Region produziert also ihre ureigene, charakteristische Verpackung. Unvergeßlich ist das Konfekt von Nagasaki, das während des *sekku*-Festes in gläsernen Dosen angeboten wird. Hübsche Flaschen in der Form eines Fisches oder einer Meereswelle als Behälter für Süßigkeiten entdeckte ich in einer Auslage von Suwa-machi. Früher gab es sie überall in Nagasaki zu kaufen, aber heute sieht man vielleicht noch zwei Varianten davon.

Ich bin gespannt, ob sich das Verpackungsdesign weiterentwickelt.

Katsu Kimura

Je devins amateur de friandises avant même de m'en apercevoir – quoique j'aime le *sake*. Il est inutile de préciser que c'est un signe de diabète. J'adore la confiserie. Je me mets à rêver dès qui je suis à proximité d'un quelconque article de confiserie.

Comme la confiserie est pleine de rêves, il va de soi que les emballages d'articles de confiserie soient eux aussi pleins de rêves.

Pour des raisons de stratégie de vente vraisemblablement, il existe comparativement peu d'emballages pour articles de confiserie chers alors qu'il existe de nombreux emballages pour confiseries de tous les jours, telles que le *Yokan* (pâte de haricots sucrée), le *Hi-gashi* (à demicru), et le *Mochi-gashi* (gâteau de riz), que l'on peut conserver pendant longtemps.

Les élégants emballages de *Kyo-gashi* (confiseries fabriquées à Kyoto) sont spécialement beaux. En ce qui concerne les *Edo-gashi* (confiseries fabriquées à Tokyo), la simplicité du district Kanto (où se situe Tokyo) se manifeste dans le gôut spécial de *l'Edo-gashi* qui diffère de celui du *Kyo-gashi*. En prenant le *Yokan* comme exemple, il me paraît intéressant de mentionner qu'on utilisait dans le temps des boîtes en fibres de bois pour les remplir de *Yokan* qui – commes les fourreaux de bambou de Kyoto – expriment bien le caractère de Edo.

Chaque district produit ses propres emballages. Les habitants de Nagasaki avaient l'habitude de garder leurs confiseries dans des bocaux de verre pendant le *sekku* (un festival saisonnier). De jolies bouteilles de confiseries en forme de poisson ou de vague comme j'en ai vu dans une devanture à Suwa-machi se vendaient partout à Nagasaki dans le temps, mais aujourd'hui, on n'en trouve guére plus que deux variations.

Je me demande si le design d'emballage va poursuire son évolution.

Katsu Kimura.

Yokan bean paste
Bohnenpaste
pâte d'haricots

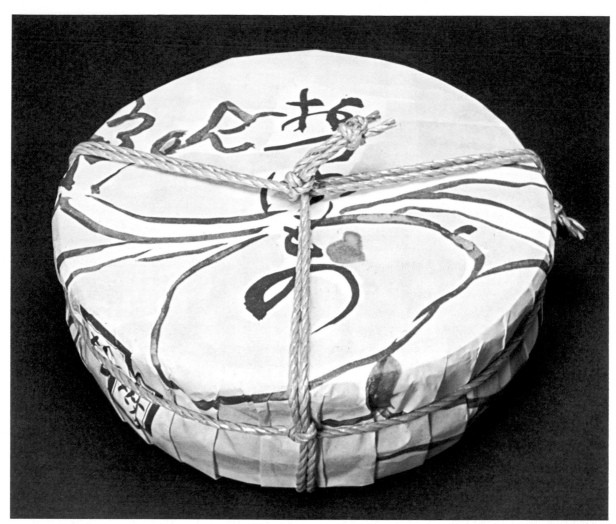

arrow root starch
Pfeilwurzstärke
fécule

rice flour
Reismehl
farine de riz

noodles
Nudeln
pâtes

18

SIMPLE AND BEAUTIFUL
EINFACH UND SCHÖN
SIMPLE ET BEAU

We went on a journey seeking packaging inspired by natural features of the regions. It was difficult to find genuine goods which made the best use of the actual locality, because there were so many urban or ubanized goods, owing to the necessity of decreasing cost by mass production or to problems in the process of distribution.

When we came to the Iwate Industrial Laboratory at Morioka we were impressed by the attitude of the staff; they applied themselves to the problem of expressing true locality, and encouraged people to make their particular products marketable as well as to publicize Iwate. Special products are *shiitake* (a kind of mushroom), walnuts, *wakame* (seaweed) and *kombu* (tangle), and they are contained in simple hand-woven bamboo bags with only tags to denote the names of the products attached. The bags are made of local and familiar material, expressing beautifully the characteristics of bamboo. It is the prerequisite of package design in cities to produce packaging with the minimum of production in order to increase productivity and economy. However, the supply of labour and natural material is abundant in Iwate, and packaging is produced at unexpectedly low cost.

As I have only dealt with the packaging design of mass-produced goods, I have a completely different idea of the design concept. As package design and the particular goods of a district are regarded as a barometer of the cultural development of the district, we now see great significance in the work of designers at the Industrial Laboratory.

Keiko Hirohashi

Wir gingen auf die Reise, auf der Suche nach Verpackungen, deren Kennzeichen die „gewachsenen" Gegebenheiten der jeweiligen Region waren. Es war schwer, authentische Produkte zu finden, bei denen die vorhandenen regionalen Eigentümlichkeiten vorteilhaft genutzt wurden. Aus der Notwendigkeit heraus, durch Massenproduktion die Kosten zu senken oder Vertriebsprobleme zu lösen, gibt es sehr viele „städtische" beziehungsweise „verstädterte" Produkte.

Als wir zu den Gewerblichen Werkstätten Iwate nach Morioka kamen, waren wir von der Auffassung der Belegschaft dort beeindruckt. Sie halten ihre Leute an, ihre Region sprechen zu lassen, wenn sie ihre Produkte marktfähig machen und für den Ort Image-Werbung betreiben wollen. Zur Produktpalette von Iwate gehören *shiitake* (Ständerpilze), Walnüsse, *wakame*-Seegras und *kombu*-Seetang. Diese Erzeugnisse werden in einfache, handgeknüpfte Bambustaschen abgepackt, mit einfachen Schildchen versehen, auf denen die Namen der Produkte stehen. Die charakteristischen Eigenschaften des Bambus kommen sehr schön zur Geltung.

In den großen Städten heißt eine der Vorgaben für das Verpackungsdesign, daß die Verpackung möglichst wenig Arbeitsgänge durchläuft, um so die Produktivität zu steigern und die Kosten zu senken. Nun, Arbeit und natürliche Rohstoffe sind in Iwate reichlich vorhanden, und Verpackungen werden daher hier mit unerwartet niedrigen Kosten produziert.

Da ich bisher ausschließlich mit dem Verpackungsdesign von Massenprodukten zu tun hatte, habe ich natürlich ein anderes Design-Konzept als das manuelle Verfahren. Da Verpackungsdesign und die charakteristischen Erzeugnisse einer Region als ein Barometer für die kulturelle Entwicklung dieser Gegend angesehen werden, kommt der Arbeit der Designer in der Gewerblichen Werkstätte eine große Bedeutung zu.

Keiko Hirohashi

Nous venons des faire un voyage à la recherche d'emballages marqués par les phénomènes naturels caractéristiques de la région d'où ils proviennent. Il était difficile de trouver des produits authentiques jouissant d'aspects caractéristiques régionaux car le souci d'en faciliter la distribution et de diminuer les coûts par une production de masse les a transformés en marchandises «urbaines» ou «urbanisées».

Quand nous sommes arrivés à l'Atelier Professionnel d'Iwate à Morioka, nous avons été impressionnés par l'attitude du personnel; il s'est voué à l'épanouissement de l'attachement des résidents à leur région. Ainsi, il montre aux gens comment rendre leurs propres produits négociables et les incite à faire de la publicité pour Iwate. Leur spécialités sont les *shiitake* (une sorte de champignons), les noix, les *wakame* (une sorte d'algue), et les *kombu* (une sorte de fucus). Tous ces produits sont empaquetés dans de simples sacs de bambou faits à la main sur lesquels sont fixées des étiquettes avec le nom des produits respectifs. Ces sacs faits en matière locale et familière sont travaillés afin de bien faire ressortir les traits caractéristiques du bambou et de les mettre joliment en valeur.

Dans les villes, une des règles de la création d'emballages est que ce dernier passe par aussi peu d'opérations que possible afin d'augmenter la productivité en diminuant les coûts. Or, à Iwate, la main d'œuvre et les matières premières abondent, ce qui explique pourquoi les emballages sont produits ici à si bon compte.

Ma conception du design est tout à fait différente de celle-ci, mais je conçois que jusqu'à lors je ne me suis occupée que du design d'emballage d'articles produits en masse. Etant donné que le design d'emballage ainsi que les produits caractéristiques d'une région sont souvent considérés comme le baromètre du développement culturel de la région en question, nous estimons que le travail des designers de l'Atelier Professionnel d'Iwate revêt une grande importance.

Keiko Hirohashi

Yam and walnuts
Yamwurzeln und Walnüsse
racines et noix

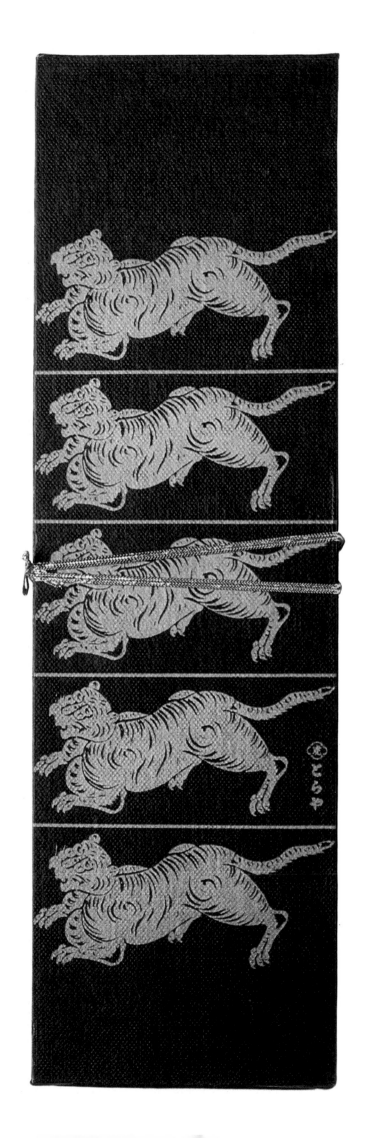

Yokan bean jelly
Yokan-Dessert
dessert Yokan

buckwheat noodles
Buchweizennudeln
pâtes de sarrasin

cookies
Gebäck
biscuits

23

SAKE

Every age has had its own type of vessel containing *sake* . *Sake* was transported in barrels in the *Edo* period and in tubs in the *Muromachi* period. A company in Osaka was the first to manufacture glass bottles. The caps of these bottles were not crown caps but corks.

The diversification of living style in the last ten years has brought with it considerable changes in the packaging of *sake*. In the past the usual form of packaging for *sake* was a 1.8 litre bottle, which used to be stored mainly in the kitchen. Now we see various kinds of packages in various places: a small bottle for a journey or a picnic, a bottle with a lovely shape for the table, and so on.

As for the material of containers, we have plastic containers in the style of bamboo, glass containers in the shape of glass by Ozeki, aluminium cans by Gekkei-Kan and paper containers. However, we cannot discuss the packaging of *sake* and exclude the 1.8 litre bottle. It was designed in the shape of a beer bottle imported at the beginning of the *Meiji* era, and yet the shape of the 1.8 litre bottle is full of beauty. A thousand brands of *sake*, distributed nationwide, are packed in bottles of the same shape. The 1.8 litre bottle has a long history of use and the advantage of low cost.

Shigeshi Ohmori

Jede Zeitperiode hatte ihre Eigenheiten, wenn es um die Abfüllung von *Sake* ging. In der *Edo*-Zeit nahm man Fässer, in der *Muromachi*-Zeit Bottiche dazu. In Osaka waren die ersten Glasflaschen in Umlauf gebracht worden. Sie hatten keine Kronenverschlüsse, sondern sie waren verkorkt wie Sekt. Die wachsende Vielgestaltigkeit der Lebensgewohnheiten während der letzten zehn Jahre hat zu großen Veränderungen in der Form der Reiswein-Abfüllung geführt. Früher war die 1,8-Liter-Flasche, die hauptsächlich in der Küche aufbewahrt wurde, die übliche Handelsform von *Sake*. Heute sieht man verschiedene Ausführungen für unterschiedlichste Gelegenheiten: die kleine *Sake*-Flasche für die Reise und das Picknick, die dekorativ gestaltete *Sake*-Flasche für die Festtafel.

Was das Material für *Sake*-Behälter betrifft, so gibt es hier Behälter aus Plastik in Bambusform, Glasbehälter von Ozeki, Aluminiumbüchsen von Gekkei-Kan sowie Papiercontainer. Wie dem auch sei, man kann nicht über das Package von *Sake* reden, ohne die 1,8-Liter-Flasche zu erwähnen. Sie wurde der Form einer zu Beginn der *Meiji*-Ära eingeführten Bierflasche nachgebildet, und noch heute hat die Form dieses Typs nichts von ihrer Schönheit eingebüßt. Die vielen verschiedenen Sorten von *Sake*, landesweit vertrieben, werden in Flaschen eben dieser Form abgefüllt. Die 1,8-Liter-Flasche hat eine lange Gebrauchstradition, und sie hat außerdem den Vorteil günstiger Abfüllkosten.

Shigeshi Ohmori

Chaque époque a eu ses particularités au niveau de la mise en tonneaux de *sake*. Pendant la période *Edo*, on utilisait des tonneaux, pendant la période *Muromachi* des cuves. C'est à Osaka que les premières bouteilles de verre furent mises en circulation. Elles n'avaient pas de capsules mais étaient fermées à l'aide de bouchons de liège.

La diversification du style de vie pendant les dix dernières années a provoqué un changement considérable de l'emballage de *sake*. Dans le passé, la présentation habituelle de *sake* était une bouteille de 1,8 litre qu'on gardait en général dans la cuisine. Aujourd'hui on observe plusieurs formes de présentation pour différentes occasions: une petite bouteille pour voyages ou pique-niques, une jolie bouteille pour la table, etc.

En ce qui concerne le matériau des conteneurs, il existe aujourd'hui des conteneurs de plastique imitant le bambou, des conteneurs de verre de Ozeki, des boîtes d'aluminium de Gekkei-Kan et des conteneurs de papier. Quoi qu'il en soit, on ne peut discuter la présentation de *sake* sans parler de la bouteille de 1,8 litre. Elle a été créée d'après la forme d'une bouteille de bière importée au début de l'ère *Meiji*, et depuis le temps, sa forme n'a rien perdu de sa beauté. Les nombreuses marques de *Sake*, distribuées à l'échelle nationale, sont toutes présentées dans des bouteilles de cette forme. La bouteille de 1,8 litre possède une longue tradition et offre l'avantage de permettre une mise en bouteilles a prix réduit.

Shigeshi Ohmori

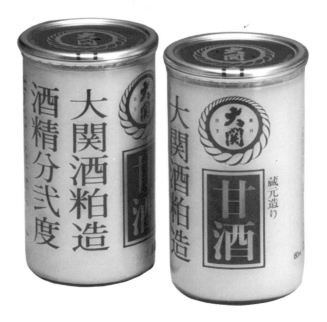

Sake wine
Reiswein
Sake

Sake wine
Reiswein
Sake

spirits
Spirituosen
spiritueux

confectionery and candies
Konfekt und Bonbons
sucreries et bonbons

Japanese tea cake
Teeplätzchen
petits gâteaux secs

33

sweets
Süßigkeiten
friandises

34

tablets of chocolate
Schokoladentafeln
tablettes de chocolat

36

Sake trade-marks
Handelsmarken von Sake
marques de Sake

登録証　第貳貳四號

要點　秀ちし丿文字

商品　第三十七種清酒

出願　明治十七年十月十一日

登録日　明治十八年六月九日

専用年限　明治三十三年六月九日迄

愛知縣下
知多郡亀崎村十六番地

平民

佐久間權七

登録証　第五貳八號

要點　八千世ノ三字

商品　第三十七種精酒

出願　明治十七年十月二日

登録日　明治十八年七月三十一日

専用年限　明治三十三年七月三十日迄

大坂府下
堺區宿院町西二丁一番地

米谷甚三郎

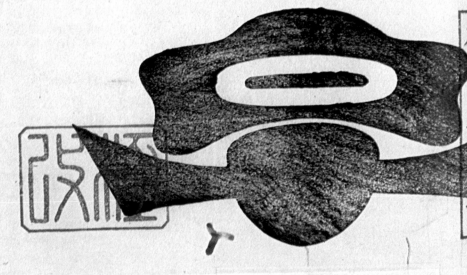

登録証　第貳參〇號

要點　白十ノ二字

商品　第三十七種醤油

出願　明治十七年十月十一日

登録日　明治十八年六月十一日

専用年限　明治三十三年六月十日迄

東京府下
深川區下大島町十五番地寄留

千葉縣平民

石川仁平治

銘酒司

本寒別造

旭

泉一

大極寒

白露

酒京三

登錄証　第八八六號

要點　旭日舞鶴波ノ圖及旭ノ文字

商品　第三十七種清酒

出願　明治三十七年十月一日

登錄日　明治三十八年十一月廿一日

專用年限　明治三十三年十一月廿日迄

三重縣下
朝明郡豐田一色村
平民
酒造業
大塚八郎兵衛

登錄証　第五貳七號

要點　泉一ノ二字

商品　第三十七種清酒

出願　明治三十七年十月三日

登錄日　明治三十八年七月三十一日

專用年限　明治三十三年七月三十日迄

大坂府下
堺區柳ノ町西一町二番地
平民
石割七左衛門

登錄証　第六〇九號

要點　白露ノ文字

商品　第三十七種清酒

出願　明治三十七年十月廿九日

登錄日　明治三十八年八月廿一日

專用年限　明治三十三年八月廿一日迄

兵庫縣下
神戶區兵庫南仲町十九番屋敷
平民
藤田サン

labels of Sake
Labels für Reiswein
vignettes de Sake

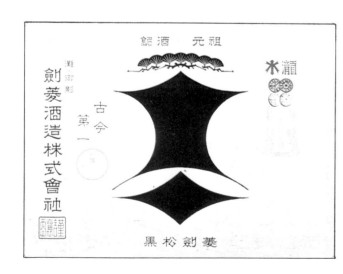

Soy trade-marks
Handelsmarken von Sojabohnenöl
marques de Soya

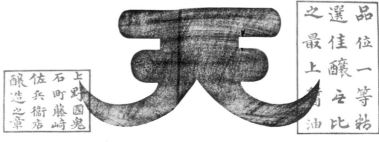

PACKAGING PRECIOUS THINGS
VERPACKUNG, DIE IHREN INHALT ACHTET
DES EMBALLAGES QUI RESPECTENT LEUR CONTENU

As cakes of soap are daily necessities and they are imperishable, they seem to be the favourite article when exchanging presents. I am given so many cakes of soap that I need not buy them. There are various ways of packing these, which, on closer inspection, may give us some insight into the designer's criteria for design and the dream he wishes to convey through his design.

I cheerfully open packages with a certain air of expectancy. Your first impression is formed by the packaging. It is etiquette to wrap things unconcernedly and modestly. We may say it is impolite to wrap things with an important and serious air. However expensive the contents may be, the sender must express through the wrapping that he considers the present a small one. Design of packaging has some restrictions; it must treat the contents as something precious; it must not stifle the contents. There are many packages which seemingly obey the restrictions but show ignorance, superficial recognition, or lack of warm consideration for the contents.

We feel grateful when we receive a present which directly conveys from the sender, his wish to send it without damaging the contents. A present which gives the impression of conceit as if the sender is shouting "This is an expensive one!", makes me feel digusted when opening it, and even reduces the value of the contents. Articles with ostentatious packaging are rarely ones of real worth.

There is a big box with a false bottom, whose inside is covered with pleated lustrous cloth. It contains only several cakes of soap. Each cake of soap is contained in a fan-shaped plastic box, wrapped in paper and laid upon a drainer in the box.

Each family has a container of soap. It is unnecessary to put each cake of soap in a little dish. The cake of soap fits so snugly into the box that it is impossible to pick it up, especially if your hand is wet. When half of the cake is used, it is, at last, possible to use the container as a soap dish. It is too absurd. I counted the wrappers from the outside: a vinyl wrapper, a paper box, two kinds of vinyl wrappers under the lid, a wooden false bottom, then artificial cloth, chemical boxes, and paraffin paper.

As we have seen, there are eight kinds of material around the cakes of soap. I have never been pro-

Da Seife eine Notwendigkeit des Alltags ist und eine unverderbliche Ware, ist sie ein geschätzter Geschenkartikel. Mir werden so viele Seifen geschenkt, daß ich keine zu kaufen brauche. Es sind die unterschiedlichsten Verpackungen, und wenn man diese genauer betrachtet, kann man die Kriterien der Designer für ihren Entwurf erkennen oder auch, welche Träume sie mit ihrem Design transportieren wollen.

Munter, mit einer gewissen Erwartung, öffne ich die Verpackungen. Die Verpackung gehört zum ersten Eindruck, den der Beschenkte erhält. Es gehört zum guten Ton, Präsente bescheiden einzupacken und so zu tun, als wäre man daran unbeteiligt gewesen. Man könnte sagen, daß es geradezu unhöflich ist, etwas auf eine wichtigtuerische und bedeutsame Art einzupacken. Wie teuer der Inhalt auch sein mag, der Geber muß in der Verpackung zum Ausdruck bringen, daß er der Ansicht ist, das Geschenk sei nur klein. Die Gestaltung einer Verpackung unterliegt gewissen Bedingungen; sie muß einerseits den jeweiligen Inhalt bestätigen und achten und darf andererseits diesen Inhalt nicht „erdrücken". Viele Verpackungen gehorchen scheinbar diesen Bedingungen, doch offenbaren sie vielfach Unkenntnis oder Unachtsamkeit oder eine mangelnde Hochachtung vor dem verpackten Inhalt.

Wir empfinden Dankbarkeit in mehrfacher Hinsicht, wenn wir ein Geschenkpäckchen bekommen, das auf direkte Weise die Gefühle des Schenkenden übermittelt, indem es in der Hoffnung übergeben wird, der Inhalt werde von seiner Verpackung nicht „erdrückt". Ein Geschenkkarton, der Überheblichkeit verrät, so, als ob der Schenkende ausriefe: „Das hier ist teuer!", stößt mich ab, und auch der Wert des Inhalts wird dadurch gemindert. Waren mit protziger Verpackung sind selten wirklich gute Waren.

Da gibt es Mogel-Kartons mit gewölbtem Doppelboden, innen ausgeschlagen mit schimmerndem, plissiertem Stoff. Der Inhalt besteht nur aus einigen Seifenstücken. Jedes davon liegt in einer fächerartig geformten Plastikbox, darin wieder in Papier gewickelt und auf einem kleinen Plastikrost ruhend.

Nun ist ja jede Familie im Besitz einer Seifendose. Es macht nicht viel Sinn, jedes Stück Seife in ein

Etant donné que les savons appartiennent aux nécessités de la vie quotidienne et qu'ils sont impérissables, ils semblent constituer des cadeaux de prédilection. On m'offre tellement de savons que je n'ai pas besoin de m'en acheter. Il y a plusieurs manières de les empaqueter et quand on examine celles-ci de façon précise, on peut y étudier les points de vue des designers à l'égard du design ou des rêves qu'ils transportent dans leur design.

J'ouvre un emballage, gai, avec une certaine espérance. C'est l'emballage qui suscite la première impression chez la personne qui reçoit un cadeau. Le bon ton exige qu'on empaquette les objets de façon modeste et comme si on n'y était pour rien. On pourrait dire qu'il est impoli d'emballer des choses de maniére importante et sérieuse. Aussi cher que soit le contenu, le donateur doit exprimer par sa façon d'emballer son présent qu'il considère que celui-ci est petit. Le design d'emballage est soumis à quelques restrictions; il est impératif qu'il respecte son contenu et le mette en valeur sans pour autant l'«écraser». Il y a des emballages qui respectent apparemment ces restrictions mais qui traduisent de l'ignorance, une connaissance superficielle, ou qui manquent de considération profonde pour leur contenu.

On se sent reconnaissant à plus d'un titre quand on reçoit un présent qu'il transmet directement le sentiment de son expéditeur qui espère que son paquet m'en «écrasera» pas le contenu. Un présent dont émane de la prétention, comme si son expéditeur criait: «Ceci est un cadeau cher!» me dégoûte, quand je me mets à l'ouvrir, et la valeur de son contenu en diminue aussi. Les articles dont l'emballage est plein d'ostentation sont en réalité rarement bons.

Il existe une grande boîte à double fond haut dont l'intérieur est recouvert de tissu plissé lustré. Elle ne contient que quelques morceaux de savon. Chaque pain de savon est placé dans une boîte en plastique en forme d'éventail, enveloppé dans du papier et posé sur un égouttoir.

Or, chaque famille possède une boîte à savon. Il est donc inutile de poser chaque morceau de savon dans une petite boîte avec un égouttoir. Le savon remplissant toute la boîte, on ne peut même pas introduire un doigt entre le savon et la paroi, et quand on a les mains mouillées, il est impossible

soap and shampoo
Seife und Haarwaschmittel
savon et shampooing

tected by eight bodyguards. I feel as if I am forced to receive these gifts with an air of profound respect.

I pick up the remains of seven or eight layers of wrapping, divide them into two groups of inflammables and non-flammables, then go down in an elevator to dispose of it. I feel miserable. Moreso, as I always try to avoid treating things roughly. Sometimes I receive a present whose contents are simply wrapped in paper and put in a box in a modest and unpretentious way. I feel the simpleness of the package. Even a sheet of paper on such a present conveys strongly the designer's feelings. My heart is softened when I encounter packages in which even a sheet of paper expresses the desirable characters of cakes of soap, such as tenderness, cleanness. I cannot throw away such sheets of paper which have absorbed the scent of cakes of soap, and put them near a mirror to re-use them. When I use them, I am reminded of the sender.

Toko Shinoda

extra Döschen zu legen. Auch ist es zu eng zwischen Seife und Rand der Seifendose, nicht einmal einen Finger breit, und mit nassen Händen kann man die Seife nicht aus der Dose herausbekommen. Ist die Hälfte des Stücks endlich aufgebraucht, kann man das Döschen als Seifendose benutzen. Das ist absurd. Ich habe einmal die Schichten der Verpackung gezählt, von außen beginnend: eine Vinyl-Einschweißbahn, der Karton aus Papier, zwei verschiedene Vinyleinlagen unterhalb des Deckels, ein zweiter Boden aus Holz, Kunstseide, die Döschen aus Kunststoff und mit Paraffin überzogenes Papier.

Wie man sieht, sind um die Seifenstücke acht verschiedene Materialien. Ich war noch nie erfreut über achtfache Schutzhäute. Mir ist, als ob ich halbseidene Prinzessinnen mit dem Ausdruck meiner größten Hochachtung empfangen müßte.

Ich sammle die Überrreste der sieben- und achtfachen Verpackungsschichten ein, unterteile sie in zwei Gruppen: brennbar oder nicht brennbar. Dann bringe ich den Abfall mit dem Aufzug hinunter. Ich fühle mich miserabel. Umso mehr, als ich immer rohe Umgangsweisen zu vermeiden suche. Manchmal erhalte ich ein Geschenk, das einfach in Papier eingeschlagen und bescheiden in eine Schachtel gelegt worden ist. Ich spüre die Schlichtheit einer solchen Verpackung. Selbst ein Streifen Papier darin kann darüber Auskunft geben, wie die Gefühle des Verpackenden beschaffen waren.

Mein Herz schmilzt dahin, wenn ich Verpackungen sehe, bei denen sogar das Blättchen Papier die wünschenswerten Eigenschaften, die man einer Seife zuschreibt, zum Ausdruck bringt, wie Zartheit, Reinheit. Ich kann diese Seifenpapiere mit dem eingefangenen Duft der Seife einfach nicht wegwerfen. Ich lege sie in die Nähe des Spiegels, um sie wieder zu benutzen. Ich denke dann an die Person, von der ich die Seife habe.

Toko Shinoda

de l'attraper. Quand le savon est à demi usé, la boîte peut enfin servir de boîte à savon. C'est absurde. J'ai compté les couches d'emballage en partant de l'extérieur: une enveloppe de vinyle, une boîte en papier, deux coussinets de vinyle différents sous le couvercle, un double fond en bois, de la soie synthétique, plusieres boîtes en matière plastique, ainsi que du papier paraffiné.

Comme nous venons de le voir, il y a donc huit différentes sortes de matériaux autour de ces morceaux de savon. Je n'ai apprécié les protections octuples. Cela me donne l'impression d'être obligé de recevoir ces princesses en fausse soie avec un air de profond respect.

Je ramasse les restes d'emballage septuple ou octuple, les divise en deux tas (inflammable ou pas), puis je prends l'ascenseur pour descendre et m'en débarrasser. Je me sens mal à l'aise. D'autant plus que j'essaie toujours de ne pas traiter les choses de façon grossière.

Parfois je reçois des cadeaux dont le contenu est simplement enveloppé dans du papier et modestement posé dans une boîte. Je suis sensible à la simplicité d'un tel emballage. Même une simple feuille de papier dans un tel cadeau en conte bien long sur les sentiments de son auteur.

Mon cœur font quand je rencontre des emballages où une seule feuille de papier exprime les caractéristiques qu'on attend d'un savon, telles que la tendresse, la pureté. Je ne peux pas jeter de telles feuilles de papier empreintes des senteurs d'un savon. Ainsi, je les pose près d'un miroir afin de les réutiliser. Et quand je m'en sers, je repense à la personne qui m'a fait cadeau du savon.

Toko Shinoda

shampoo
Haarwaschmittel
shampooing

tablets of soap
Seifenstücke
pains de savon

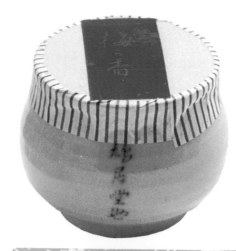

incense
Räucherwerk
encens

AVANTGARDE

SHIGERU AKIZUKI
TAKASHI KANOME
TOSHIO SUGIMURA
KATSU KIMURA
U. G. SATO
KOZO OKADA
AKIKO ARAI
RYO ARAI
KEIKO HIROHASHI

秋月繁

The Relieving Touch of Wood.

Wood has warmth. It is solid to the touch but delicate to look at.

Each tree has its own fragrance and lustre and color, a kind of personality. The drawers in the shape of a Bodhidharma doll which I made three years ago still shed the fragrance of Japanese cypress when a drawer is opened.

I made an envelope out of paulownia, making use of its lightness.

Bodhidharma dolls, playful boxes of folk masks and drawers, gift packaging for cakes and liquor bottles . . . these are all made of pine, cedar or plywood.

Wood is cut, painted, silk-screen processed or hand-painted. I am happy if customers feel relaxed when looking at our wood packaging.

Das Entspannende von Holz.

Holz hat Wärme. Es fühlt sich robust an, wenn man es berührt, doch es sieht sehr empfindlich aus.

Jeder Baum hat seinen eigenen Wohlgeruch, seinen eigenen Glanz, seine eigene Farbe, etwas von Persönlichkeit. Die Kommode in Form einer Bodhi-Dharma-Puppe, die ich vor drei Jahren gemacht habe, strömt beim Öffnen einer Schublade noch heute den Duft von japanischen Zypressen aus.

Ich habe aus dem Holz der Paulownie ein Briefkuvert gemacht und habe dabei dessen geringes Gewicht ausgenutzt.

Bodhi-Dharma-Puppen, verspielte Kästchen mit volkstümlichen Masken und Schubfächern, Geschenkkartons für Kuchen und Likörflaschen . . . all dies wird aus Pinie, Zeder oder Furnierholz gefertigt.

Holz wird geschnitten, von Hand bemalt oder im Siebdruckverfahren gefärbt. Ich freue mich, wenn Abnehmer sich entspannen können beim Betrachten unserer Holzkästchen.

L'effet reposant du bois.

Le bois est chaud. Il est ferme au toucher mais très fragile d'aspect.

Chaque arbre a son propre parfum, son propre lustrage, sa propre couleur; une sorte de personnalité. La commode en forme de poupée Bodhi-Dharma que j'ai créée il y a trois ans répand encore le parfum du cyprès japonais quand on en ouvre les tiroirs.

J'ai fait une enveloppe en bois Paulownia, mettant ainsi à profit sa légèreté.

Les poupées Bodhi-Dharma, les boîtes gaiement enjolivées de masques folkloriques et les tiroirs, les cartons-cadeaux pour gâteaux et les bouteilles de liqueurs . . .

tout cela est fait en pin, en cèdre ou en contre-plaqué.

On coupe, peint, embellit le bois à l'aide du procédé de sérigraphie ou en le peignant à la main. Je me réjouis quand un acheteur se détend à la vue de nos emballages de bois.

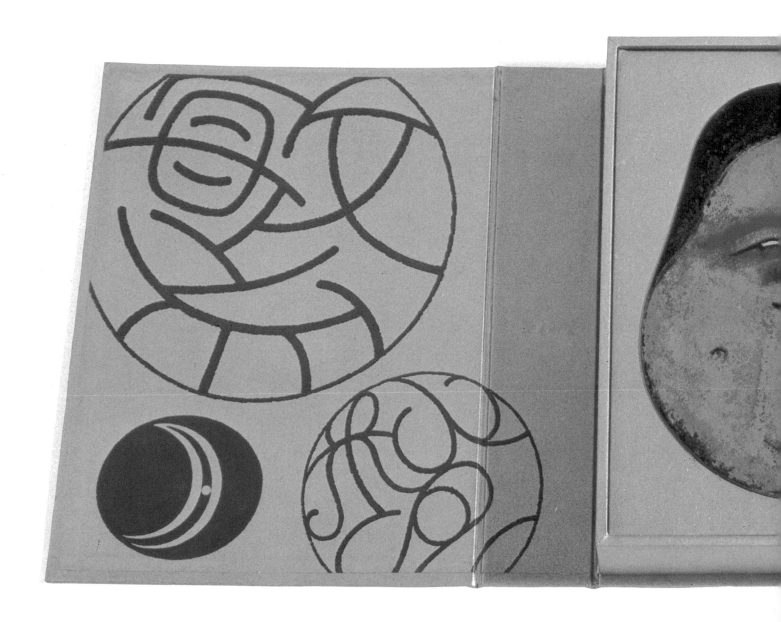

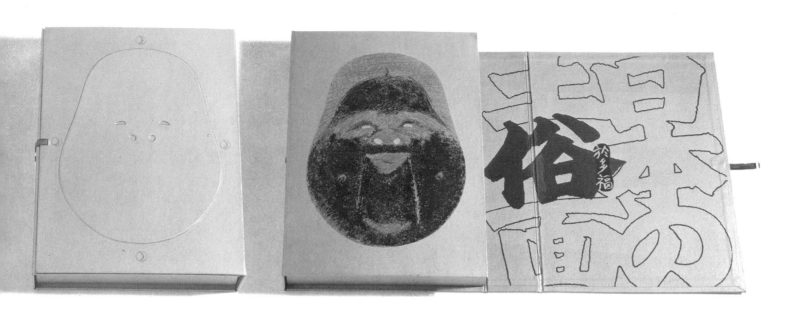

秋月繁

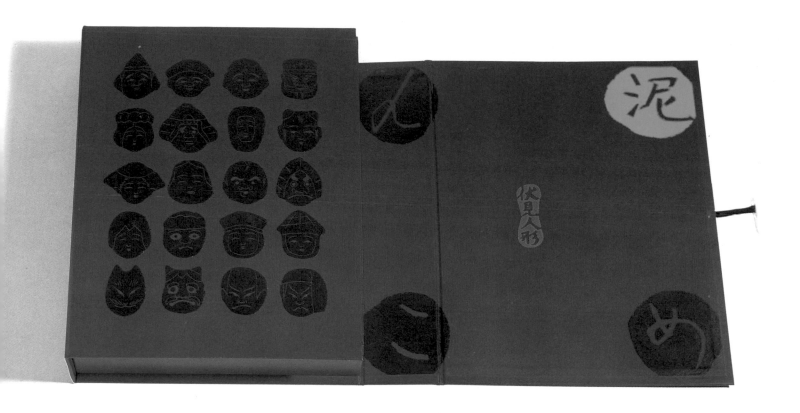

61

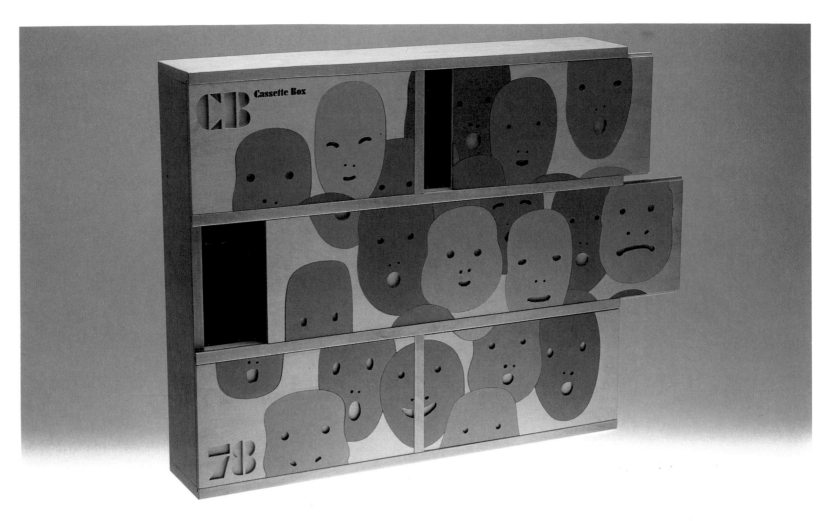

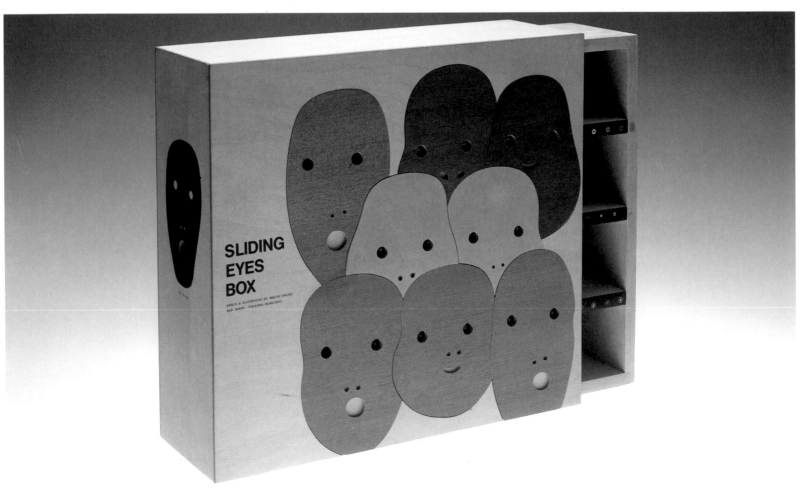

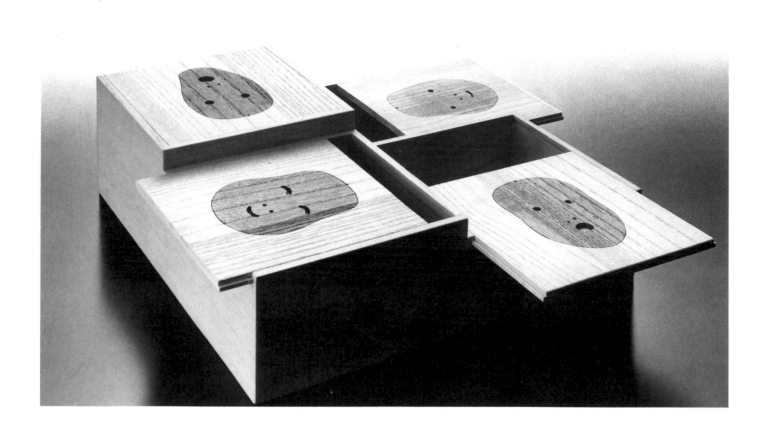

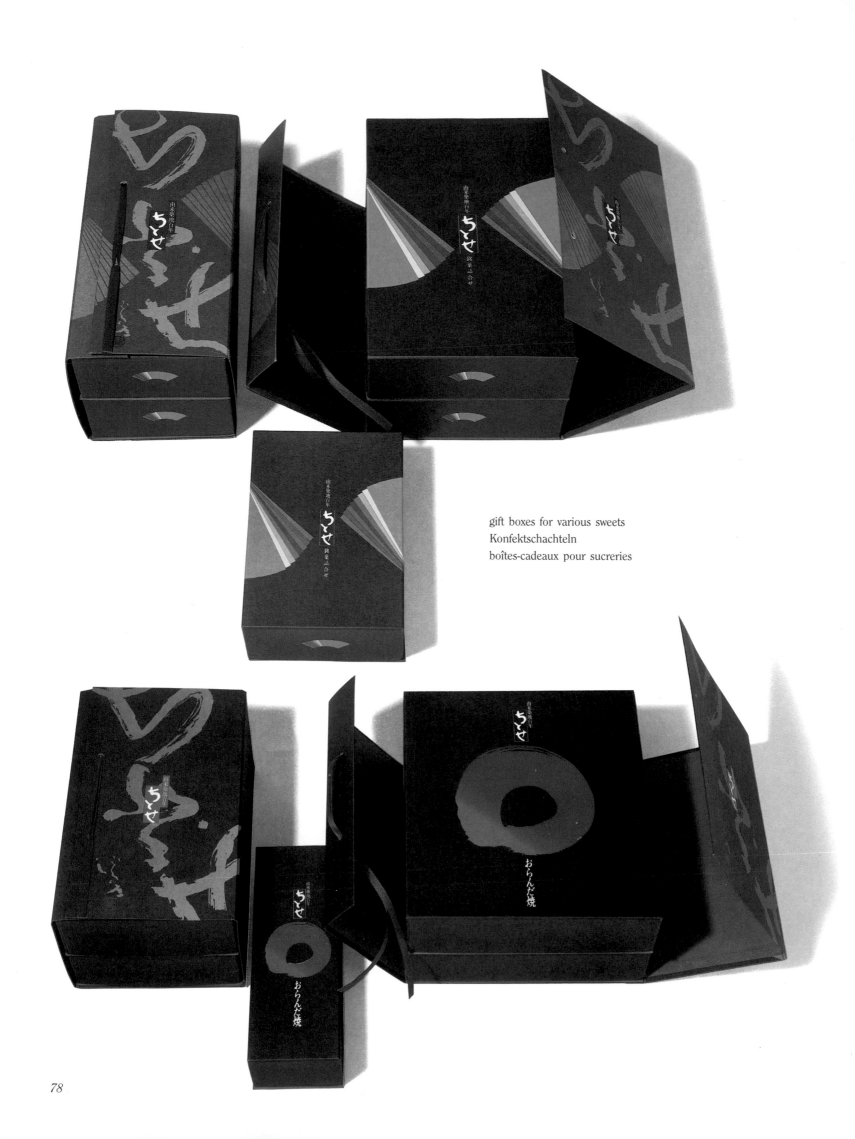

gift boxes for various sweets
Konfektschachteln
boîtes-cadeaux pour sucreries

set of cans and containers for soft confection
Dreierset für halbrohes Konfekt
set en trois parties pour confiserie à demi crue

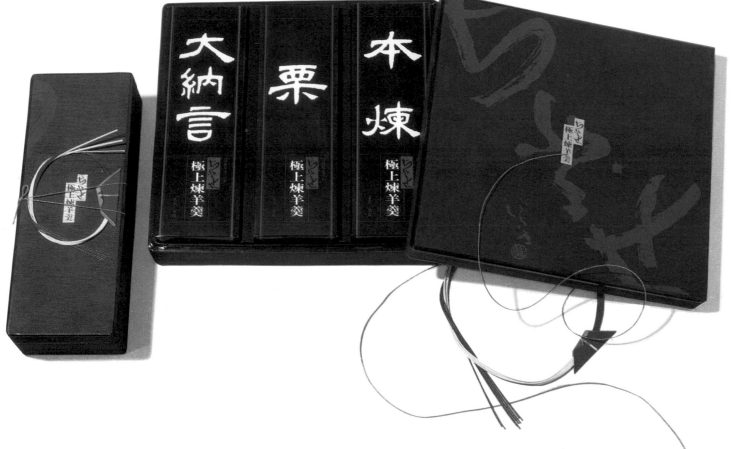

Shopping bags
Tragetaschen
sacs

鹿目尚志

TAKASHI KANOME

I feel the hugeness and the fearfulness of the act of wrapping. When you think in terms of the universe, life and living, you find that everything just gets wrapped up.
But when I stop to think I am involved in the indecent work of wrapping things up every day, when I have a chance to do a piece of work any way I please, I find myself wanting to search for the starting point of this fear.
The readiness to seal, tie up, and enclose whenever I get the chance is an expression of my search and the fear I find there. The thing that struggles to escape from my work —
is myself.

My image box is a folding book box filled with traditional Japanese folk masks and toys. I have planned a sequence of events, both unexpected and autonomous, which is set in motion when the first lid is opened and followed by by the second lid being opened.

Ich empfinde das Kolossale und die Ungeheuerlichkeit, die im Vorgang des Verpackens liegen. Wenn man in den Kategorien des Universiums, der Existenz und des Lebens denkt, dann kann man zu dem Schluß kommen, daß letzten Endes alles und jedes verpackt wird. Doch wenn ich aufhöre daran zu denken, daß ich tagtäglich an dem anstößigen Werk, Dinge zu verpacken, beteiligt bin, wenn ich die Möglichkeit habe, etwas so zu gestalten, wie ich es für richtig halte, dann möchte ich nach dem Ausgangspunkt für diese angstvolle Empfindung suchen.
Die Bereitschaft, etwas zu versiegeln, zu verschließen und zu verschnüren, wann immer es geht, ist Ausdruck meiner Suche und der Angst, auf die ich dabei treffe. Die Materie, die sich qualvoll von meinen Arbeiten befreien möchte – das bin ich selbst.

Meine Bilder-Schachtel ist eine Falt-Buch-Schachtel mit traditionellen, volkstümlichen japanischen Masken und Gesellschaftsspielen. Ich habe die Unvorhersehbarkeit und die Eigengesetzlichkeit eines aufeinander aufbauenden Geschehens geplant, das in Gang kommt, wenn erst der obere Deckel und dann der Innendeckel geöffnet wird.

J'éprouve la colossalité et la monstruosité qui résident dans le processus de l'emballage. Quand vous méditez sur des termes tels que «l'univers», «l'existence», où bien «la vie», vous arrivez à la conclusion qu'en fin de compte, on empaquette pratiquement tout.
Mais quand je cesse de songer au fait que je participe chaque jour à cette corvée répugnante consistant à empaqueter toutes sortes d'objets, quand j'ai la possibilité d'aborder un travail d'une façon qui me plaît, j'ai toujours grande envie de chercher l'origine de cette peur.
Ma disposition à cacheter, enfermer ou ficeler dès que cela est possible trahit ma quête et la peur que j'y rencontre. La matière qui se torture pour se libérer de mon œuvre – c'est moi-même.

Ma boîte à images est une boîte à livre pliante remplie de masques folkloriques traditionnels japonais et de jeux. J'ai projeté l'imprévisibilité et l'autonomie d'un développement successif qui se révèle quand on ouvre d'abord le couvercle supérieur de la boîte et ensuite sa couverture intérieure.

28 handles to one side making a total
of 112 handles for the four sides.
28 Hebel auf einer Seite ergeben
zusammen 112 Hebel für vier Seiten.
28 leviers de chaque côté font en tout
112 leviers pour quatre côtés.

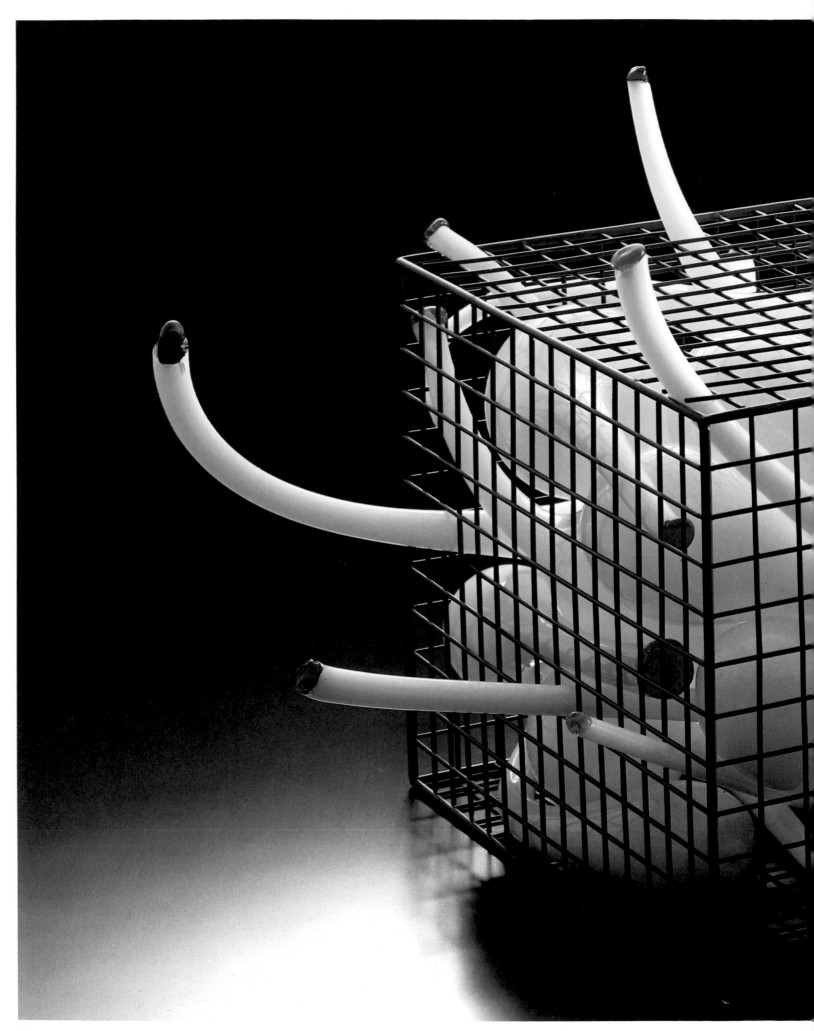

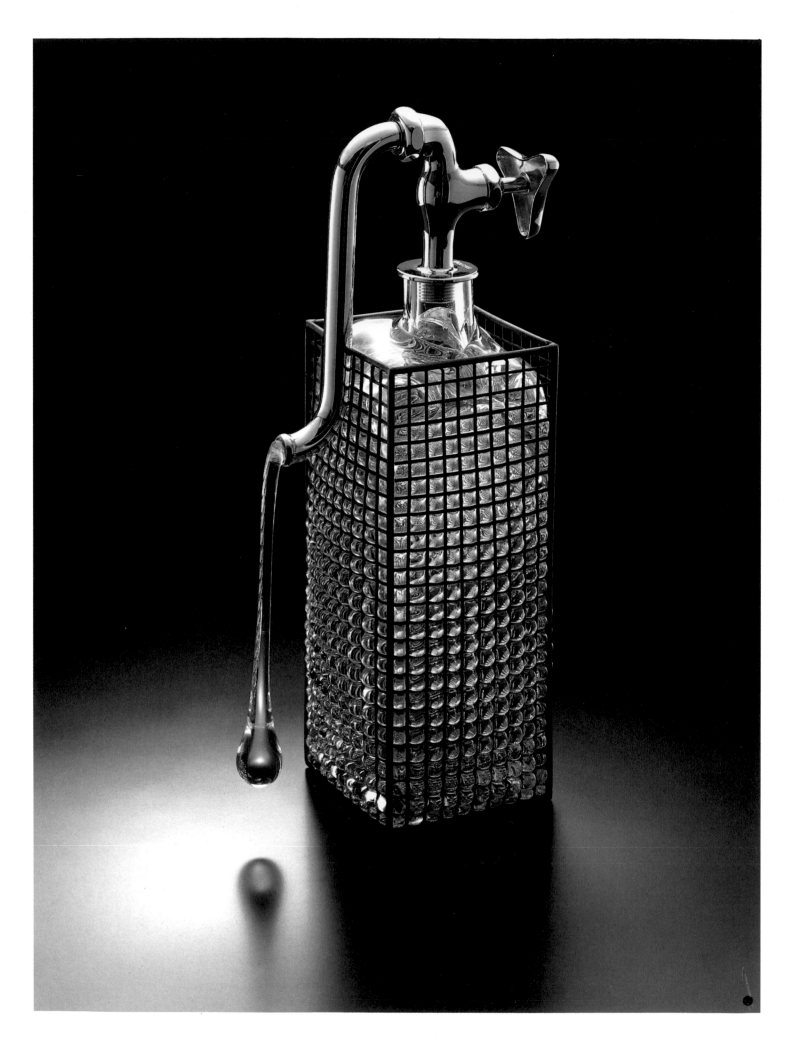

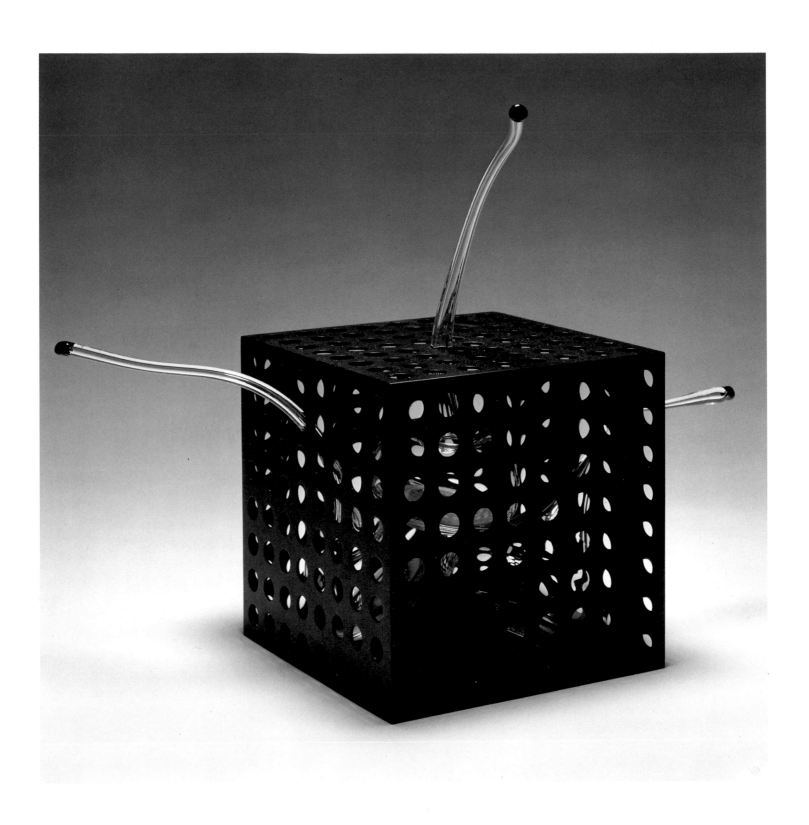

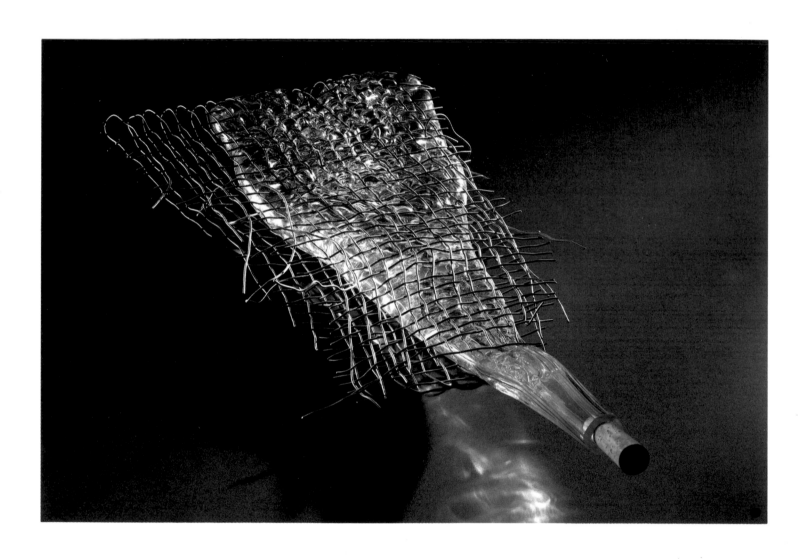

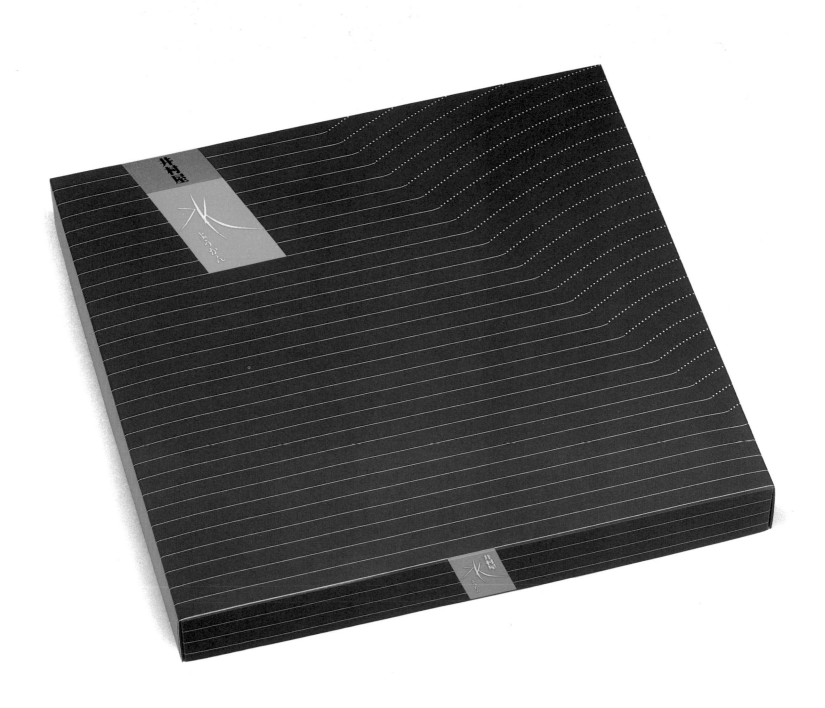

confectionery boxes
Konfekt-Schachteln
boîtes de confiserie

100

shopping bag
Tragetasche
sac

Sweet bean paste
rote Bohnenpaste
pâte de haricots

杉村敏男

TOSHIO SUGIMURA

Re-using Boxes.

There are lots of surprises and impressive happenings in today's fast moving world. I often feel flurried by the rapid pace of change. Each piece of my collection of tin toys, money-boxes and bottles made during and right after World War II has a special naive and artless taste reflecting the time of production.

Some of the packaging made in earlier years has disappeared but no one cares about it. Companies with a long-standing history change their names and introduce a whole new corporate identity concept in their publicity and packaging.

In the world of commercialism, there is an illusion that novelty is the essence of design. That is not correct. I personally find dignity in old things. I would like to devote myself to handling wood, making boxes and drawers that can be used again and again.

Kästchen im ständigen Gebrauch.

In der rastlosen Welt von heute gibt es eine Menge Überraschungen und beeindruckende Ereignisse. Ich fühle mich oft beunruhigt von der Schnelligkeit des Wandels. Jedes Stück meiner Sammlung von Blechspielzeug, Spardosen und Flaschen, die ich in der Zeit während und nach dem Zweiten Weltkrieg angelegt habe, hat einen besonderen naiven und ungekünstelten Anspruch, in dem sich die Zeit seiner Herstellung widerspiegelt.

So manche Verpackung aus den frühen Jahren ist verlorengegangen, doch das kümmert niemanden. Handelshäuser mit einer langen Firmengeschichte ändern ihre Namen und führen ein ganz neues Erscheinungsbild für Werbung und Verpackung ein.

In der Welt des Kommerzes gibt es eine Illusion, wonach das Wesen des Design die Novität ist. Ich finde das falsch. Ich persönlich erkenne Würde in alten Gegenständen. Ich befasse mich gern mit Holz, mache Kästchen und Schubladen daraus, denn sie werden immer wieder benutzt.

La réutilisation des boîtes.

Dans le monde d'aujourd'hui où règne la vitesse, il y a beaucoup de surprises et d'événements impressionnants. La vitesse du changement me préoccupe souvent. Chaque pièce de la collection de jouets tôle, de tirelires et de bouteilles, que j'ai réunie pendant et après la Seconde Guerre mondiale, a un caractère très naïf et naturel dans lequel se reflète l'époque de sa fabrication.

Une partie des emballages datant des premières années ont disparu, mais personne ne s'en préoccupe. Des compagnies jouissant d'une longue tradition changent de nom et introduisent une image d'elles-mêmes totalement neuve dans leur publicité et leurs emballages.

Dans un monde marqué par le commercialisme, on nourrit l'illusion que la nouveauté constitue l'essence du design. Ce n'est pas le cas. Personellement, je trouve de la dignité aux vieux objets. J'aime bien m'adonner à travailler le bois, à en faire des boîtes et des tiroirs, car on peut sans cesse les réutiliser.

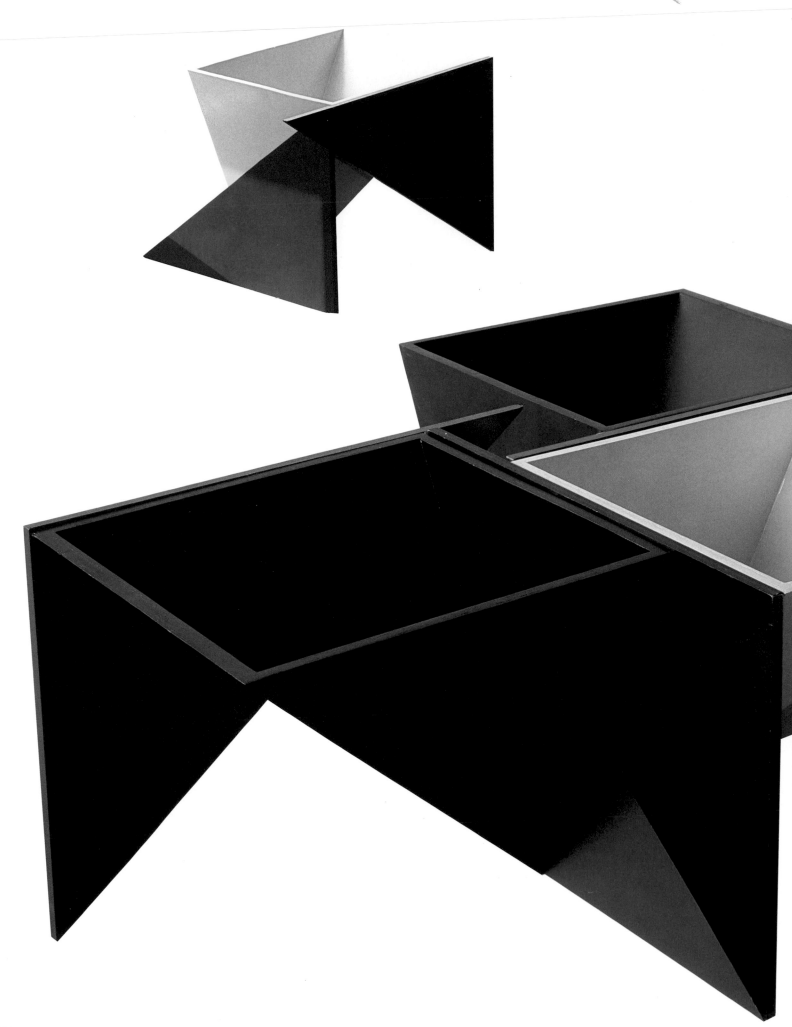

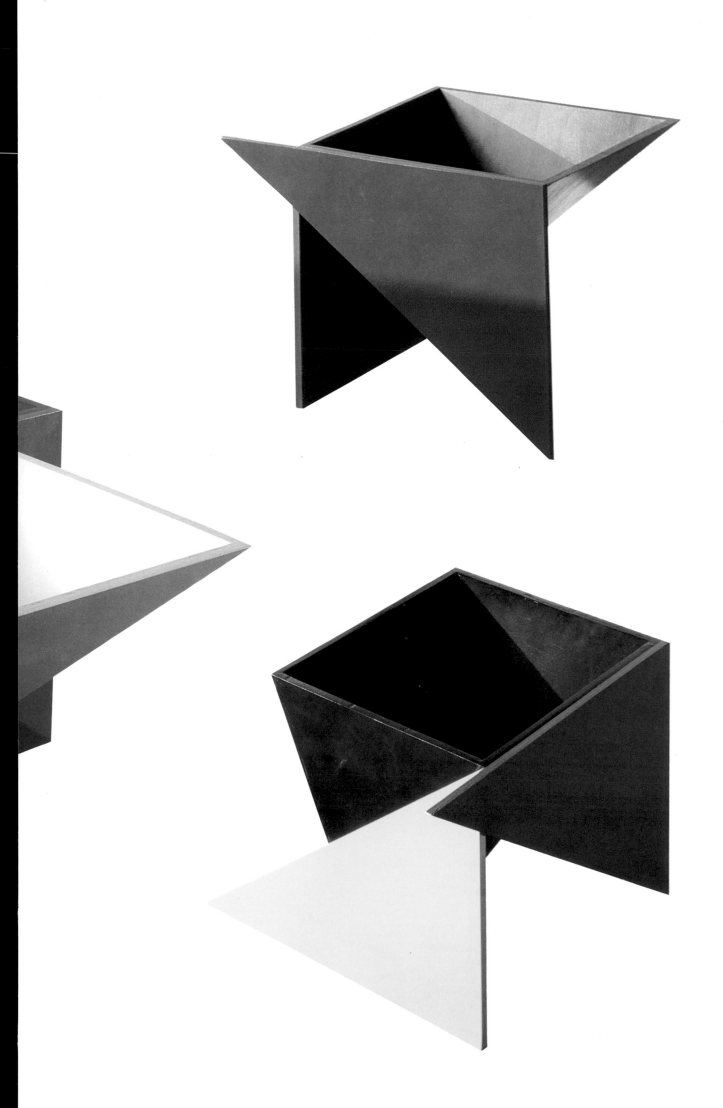

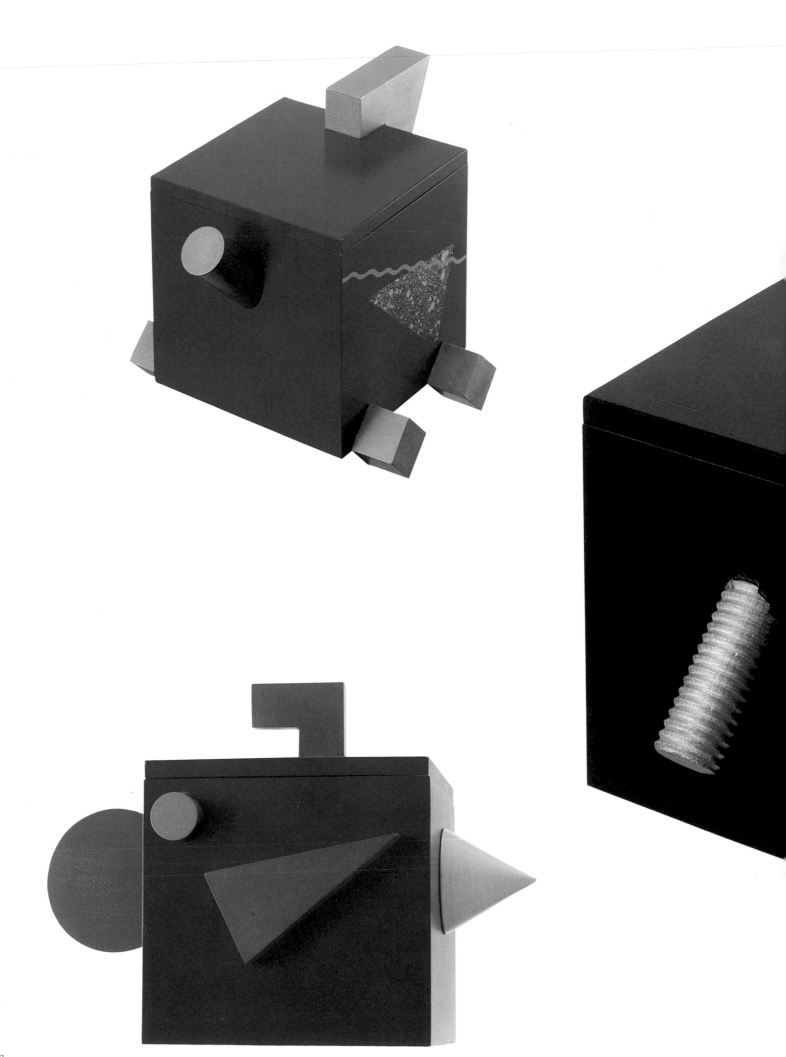

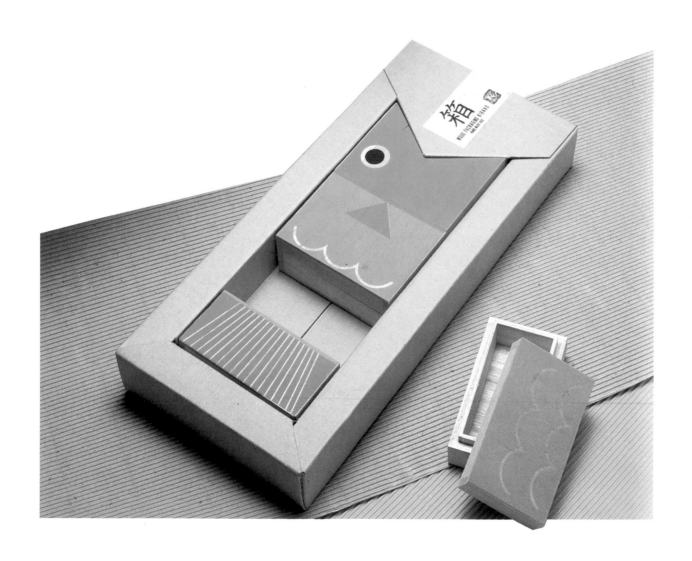

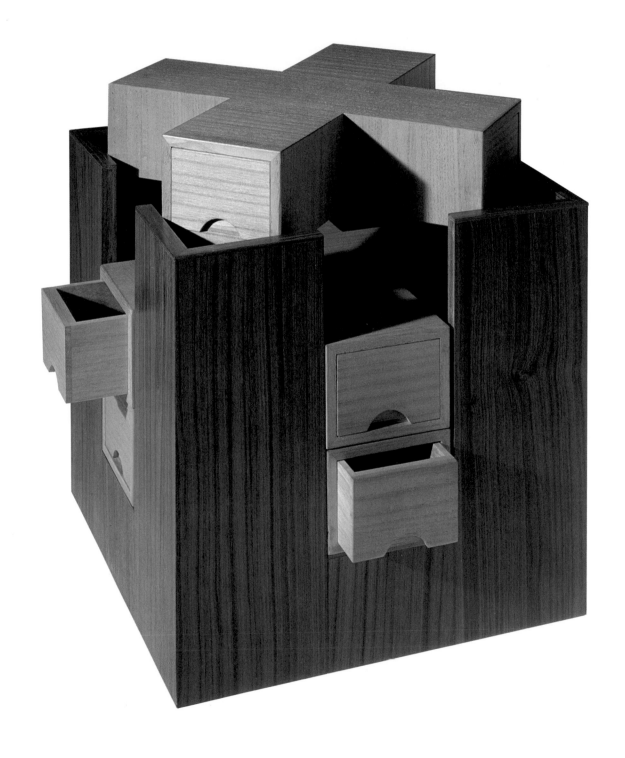

木村勝

KATSU KIMURA

A box that is not paper
that will not be torn
that will not be thrown away
that has no purpose
no meaning and no value.
The fate of the things inside
will be decided by the box itself.

Eine Schachtel, nicht mehr aus Papier
die nicht zerrissen wird
die keinen Zweck erfüllt
keine Funktion und keine Bedeutung hat.
Über das Schicksal der Gegenstände
in ihrem Innern
wird die Schachtel selber entscheiden.

Une boîte qui n'est plus papier
qui ne sera pas déchirée
qui ne sera pas jetée, qui n'a aucun but
aucune importance, ni aucune valeur.
C'est la boîte elle-même qui décidera
du sort des objets
qu'elle contient.

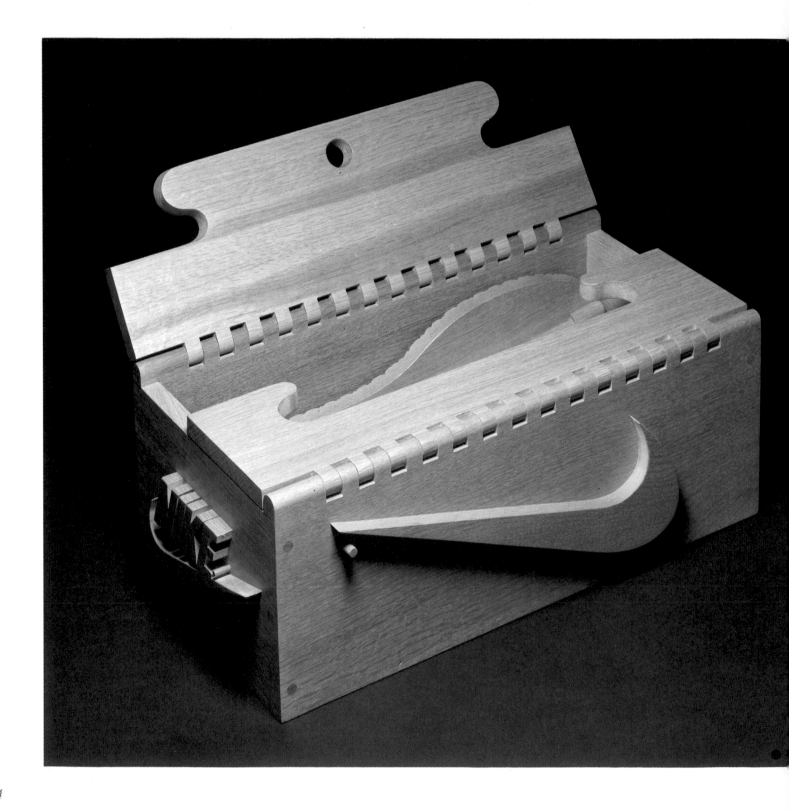

115

waste-paper basket
Papierkörbe
corbeilles à papier

bags
Einkaufstüten
sacs

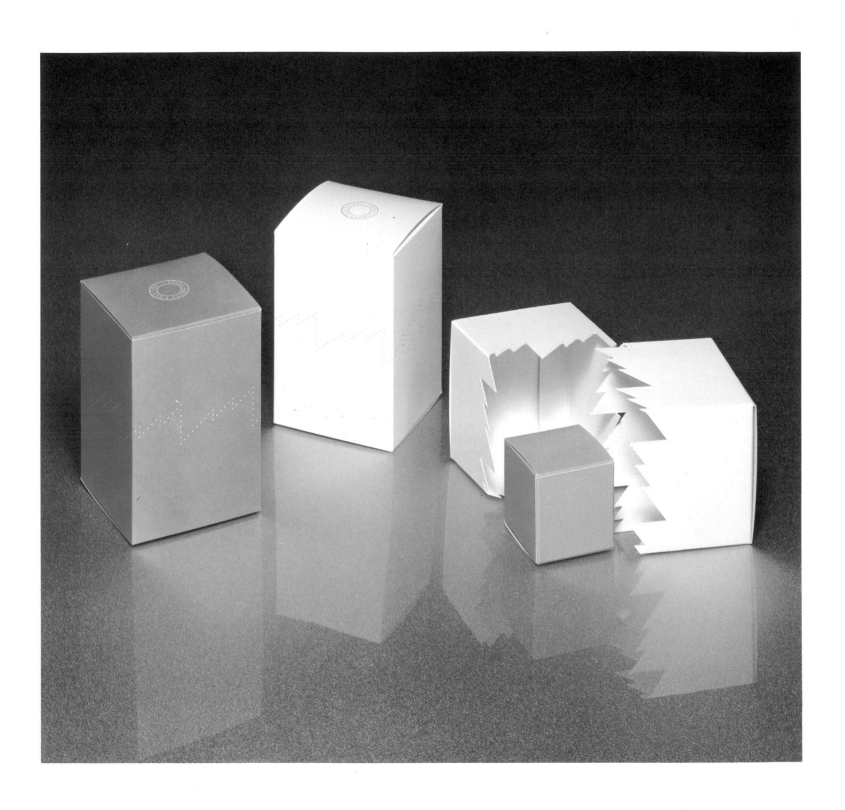

crackers
Kräcker
biscuits

boxes for sweets
Konfektschachteln
boîtes pour sucreriers

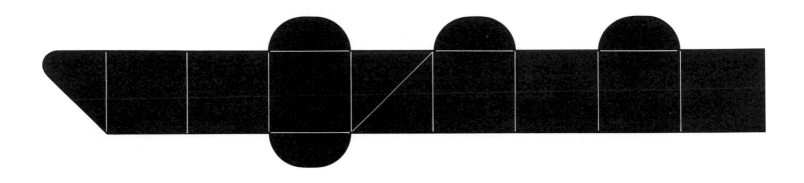

reversible box
beidseitig bedruckte Box
boîte imprimée des deux côtés

gift boxes
Geschenkkartons
boîtes-cadeaux

123

dispenser
Verkaufshilfe
dispensateur

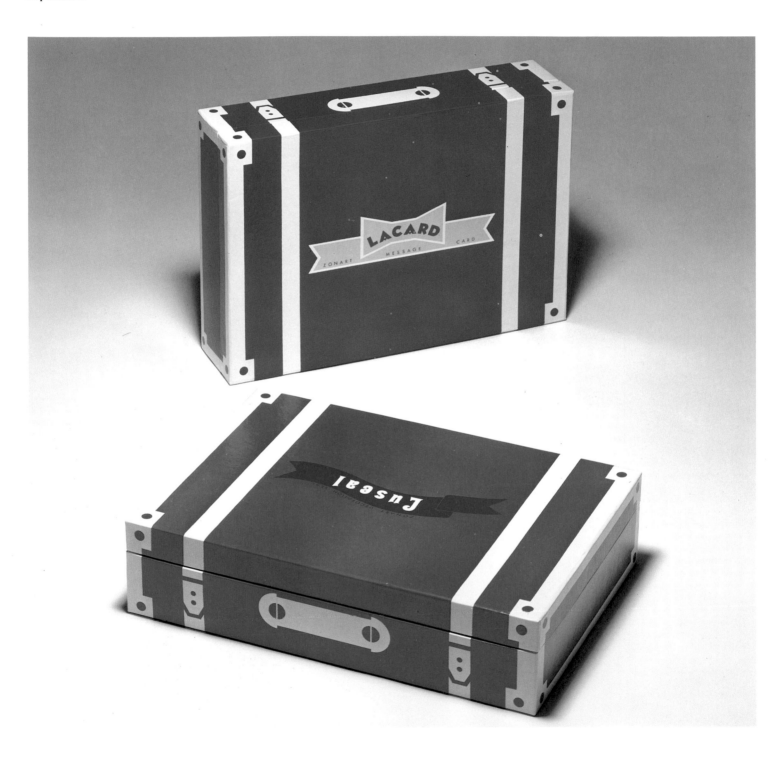

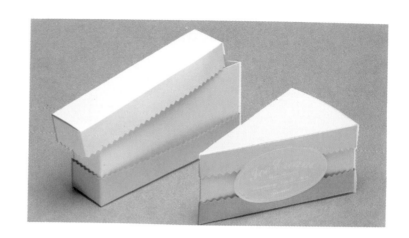

cake box
Kuchenschachtel
boîte à gâteau

gift box
Geschenkkarton
boîte-cadeaux

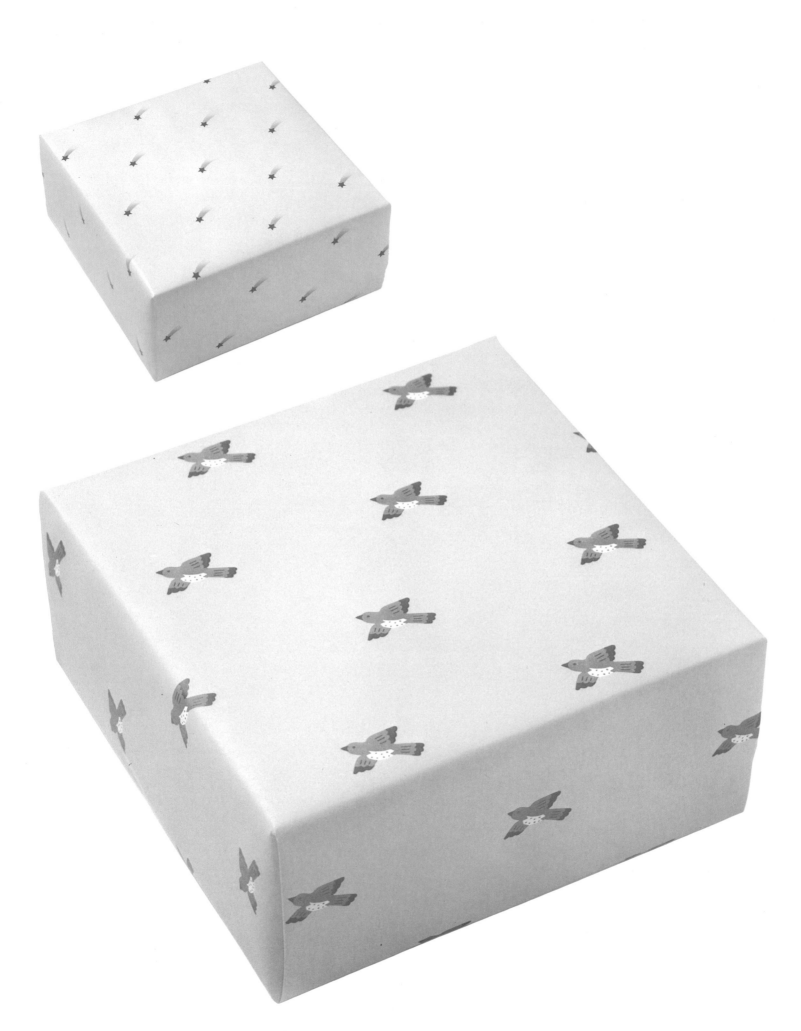

U.G.サトー

U. G. SATO

From a Closed World to an Open World.
Pack, tuck away, hide away, treasure.
A strong image clings to the box. It is even
more so with a box made of wood because of its
image of solidity and long-life.
My crabbed sensitivity rises in revolt to escape
from conventional impressions and to take flight
into a different space. Thus, I introduce the
nonsensical "trompe l'oeil" that I often use in
my illustration work, employing two-dimensional
methods in three-dimensional thoughts.
It will be a success if this trick technique can
cause a little surprise or even a smile among
viewers. I am pleased if the closed and heavy
world turns into an open and light world.

Aus einer verschlossenen zu einer offenen Welt.
Packe, verstaue, verstecke, sammle.
Mit einem Kästchen verbinden sich intensive
Vorstellungen. Dies gilt umso mehr für ein
Kästchen aus Holz wegen seiner Festigkeit und
Langlebigkeit.
Meine Sensibilität erhebt sich gegen
konventionelle Einflüsse und setzt zum Flug
an in andere Räume. So habe ich das Unsinns-
„tromp-l'oeil" eingeführt, das in meinem
graphischen Werk oft zur Anwendung kommt;
ich gebrauche dabei zweidimensionale Methoden
in dreidimensionalen Gedanken. Es ist ein Er-
folg für mich, wenn diese Tricktechnik beim
Betrachter ein wenig Irritation auslöst oder gar
ein Lächeln bewirkt. Es freut mich, wenn sich
die verschlossene und lastende Welt in eine
offene und lichte Welt verwandelt.

D'un monde clos vers un monde ouvert.
Emballe, case, cache, amasse.
Une forte image colle à la boîte. Ceci est
d'autant plus valable pour une boîte en bois, à
cause de son caractère de solidité et de longue
vie.
Ma sensibilité s'échauffe, se révolte contre les
influences conventionnelles pour s'envoler vers
d'autres espaces. Ainsi, j'ai introduit cet insensé
«trompe-l'œil» que j'utilise souvent dans mes
illustrations, et applique des méthodes bidimen-
sionnelles à des idées tridimensionnelles. C'est
une victoire pour moi quand cette technique
astucieuse provoque un peu de perplexité ou
même un sourire parmi le public. Il me plaît
que le monde clos et lourd se transforme en un
monde ouvert et clair.

136

岡田宏三

KOZO OKADA

Boxes for Visual Communication.

These boxes go along with my recent design theme of having one object with two hidden subjects. The object is "the world of visual dialogue", which means designing packages as pieces of communication with consumers.

One of the subjects is "re-discovering the texture of the material", or exploring a new touch to the conventional packaging materials which have made a limited visual impression. The other subject is "the form of entertainment". When a space for visual dialogue is to be composed, a desire to entertain is needed.

I am confident that if a designer can enjoy designing a package with a fresh feeling towards the material, inspiration comes naturally. Instead of designing wooden packages that viewers can "understand", the theme of my package design is for the viewers to feel something.

My recent works can be categorized, material-wise, into the following:

1. Stripe Wood Package. Slender pieces of square timber with different textures are arranged at random and lined, thus enabling the use of a curved face.

2. Cut Wood Package. Small headers are composed to create a new impression of the material.

3. Sliced Wood Package. Wooden foils of different texture are composed to make packaging composed of both wood and paper.

Kästchen zur visuellen Kommunikation.

Die Kästchen setzen ein Thema meiner letzten Arbeiten fort – ein Objekt mit zwei Motiven. Das Objekt heißt „die Welt des visuellen Dialogs", das bedeutet: Verpackung zu gestalten als Bindeglied zur Verständigung mit dem Verbraucher.

Eines der beiden Motive ist die „Wieder-entdeckung der Materialstruktur"; wobei es darum geht, ein neues Gefühl für die herkömmlichen Verpackungsmaterialien zu entwickeln, die für den Betrachter nur eine beschränkte Ausdrucksfähigkeit haben. Das andere Motiv ist die „Form der Unterhaltung". Zur Gestaltung von Raum für den visuellen Dialog braucht man Sinn für Unterhaltung.

Wenn es einem Designer Spaß macht, eine Verpackung mit Gefühl für das verwendete Material zu entwerfen, dann bin ich zuversichtlich, daß sich entsprechende kommunikative Inspiration von selbst einstellt. Statt Verpackungen aus Holz zu gestalten, die der Betrachter „versteht", habe ich es mir zur Aufgabe gemacht, Verpackung so zu gestalten, daß man beim Betrachten etwas empfindet.

Meine jüngsten Arbeiten lassen sich anhand des Materials folgendermaßen klassifizieren:

1. Verpackungen aus Streifenholz: Schmale Stücke aus quadratischem Schnittholz mit voneinander abweichender Maserung werden nach dem Zufallsprinzip oder aber ganz bewußt zusammengestellt, wodurch eine gekrümmte Oberfläche entsteht.

2. Verpackungen aus geschnittenem Holz: Kleine Verbindungsstücke werden so zusammengesetzt, daß ein neuer Materialeindruck entsteht.

3. Verpackungen aus Holzblattwerk: Folien mit verschiedenartiger Maserung werden so zusammengestellt, daß eine Packung entsteht, deren Material zur Hälfte aus Holz, zur anderen Hälfte aus Papier besteht.

Des boîtes pour la communication visuelle.

Les boîtes présentées traitent un sujet qui m'avait déjà préoccupé dans mes dernières œuvres – présenter un objet qui incorpore deux sujets. L'objet, c'est «la vie du dialogue visuel», consistant à façonner les emballages de telle façon qu'ils deviennent un élément de communication avec le consommateur.

L'un des deux sujets se nomme «redécouverte de la texture des matériaux» ou autrement dit la quête d'une nouvelle conception des matériaux d'emballage conventionnels, dont la vue ne génère qu'une impression limitée. L'autre sujet est intitulé «forme de divertissement», quand un espace doit être composé pour le dialogue visuel, on a besoin d'un esprit ouvert au divertissement.

Si un designer trouve plaisir à créer un emballage sans faire preuve d'idées préconçues à l'égard de la matiére qu'il utilise, je suis persuadé que l'inspiration correspondante apparaîtra d'elle-même. Au lieu de créer des emballages en bois que le public «comprend», le thème de ma démarche est de créer des emballages de telle façon que le public éprouve quelque chose en les regardant.

Mes œuvres récentes peuvent être classées, en fonction de la matière que j'y utilise, à savoir:

1. Emballage de bandes de bois. Morceaux de bois minces de madrure variée, arrangés selon le principe du hasard on tout à fait consciemment, afin de créer une surface extérieure bombée.

2. Emballage en bois scié. Petites jointures composées de telle façon qu'elles donnent une nouvelle impression de la matière.

3. Emballage en bois coupé en disques. Feuilles de bois de madrure variée, composées de telle façon qu'il en résulte un emballage dont la matière oscille entre le bois et le papier.

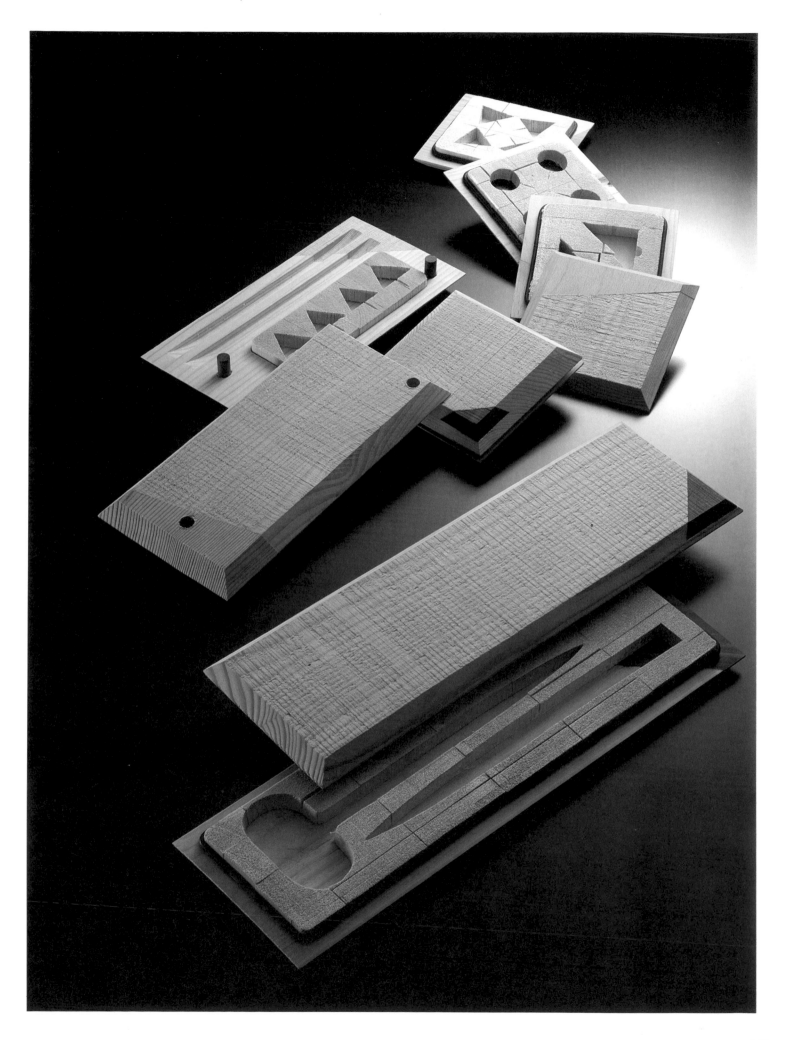

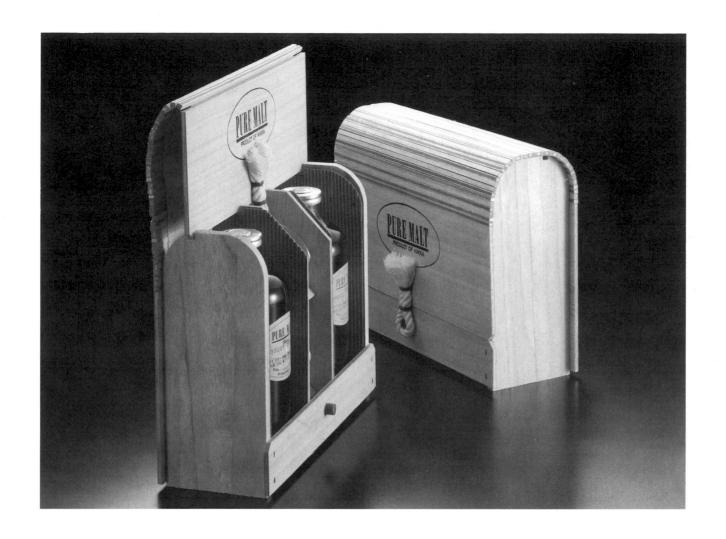

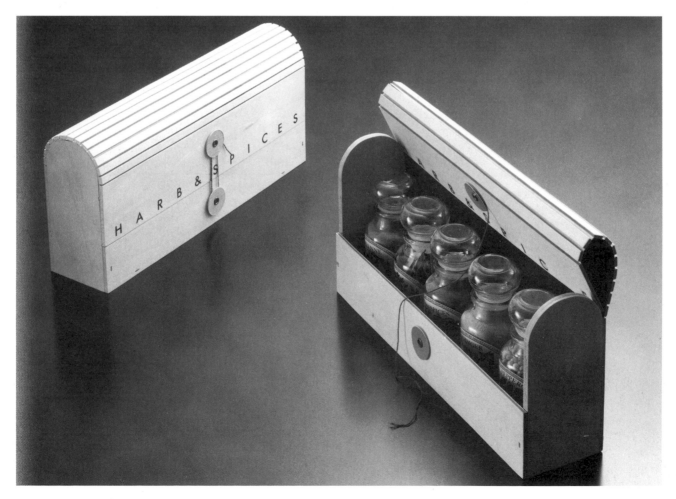

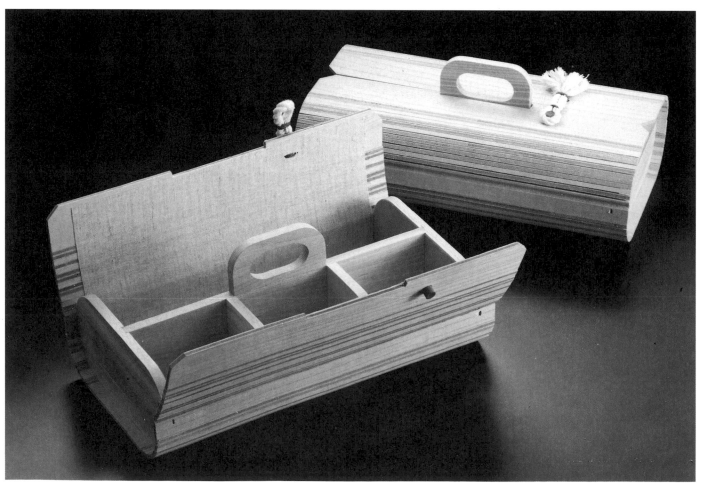

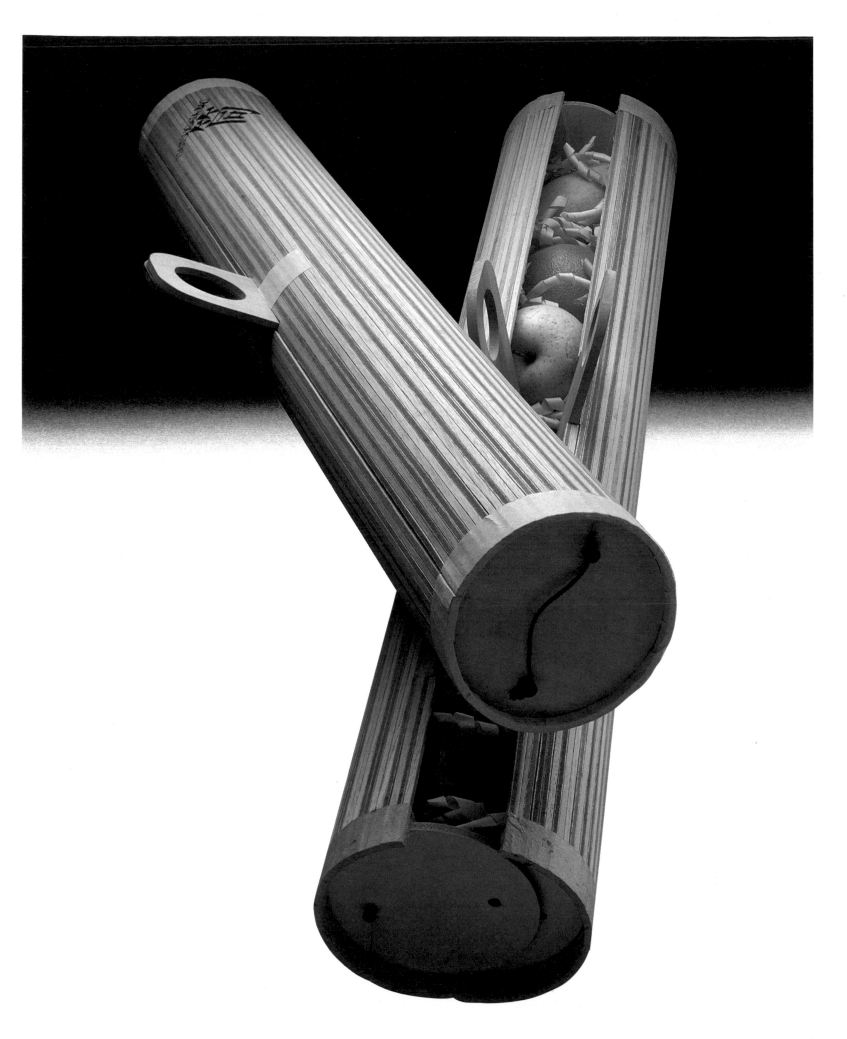

九拾壱
Gallery 91

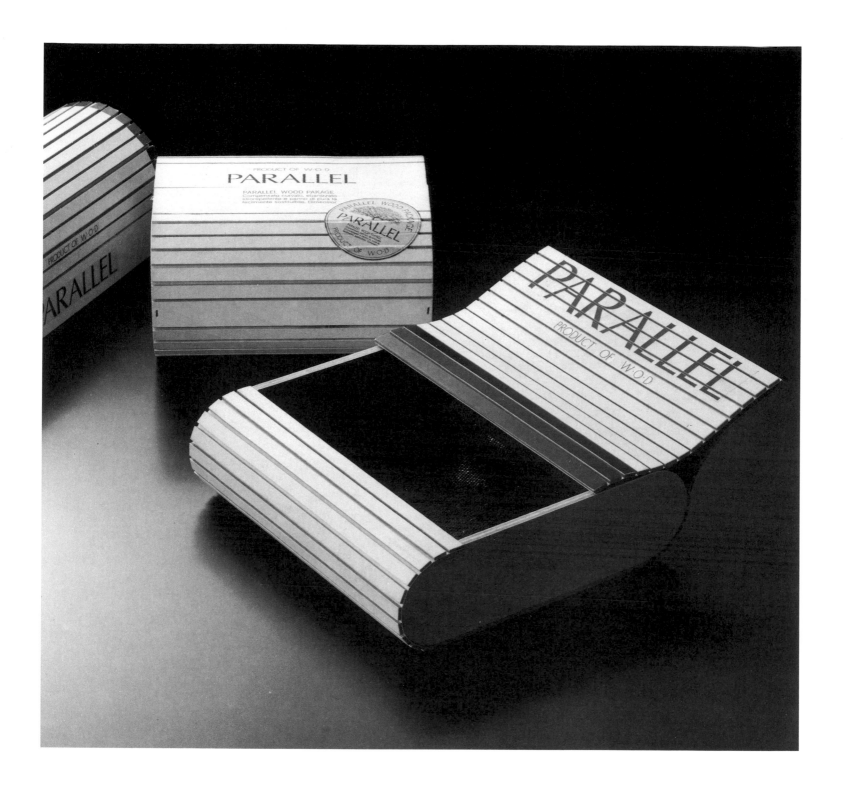

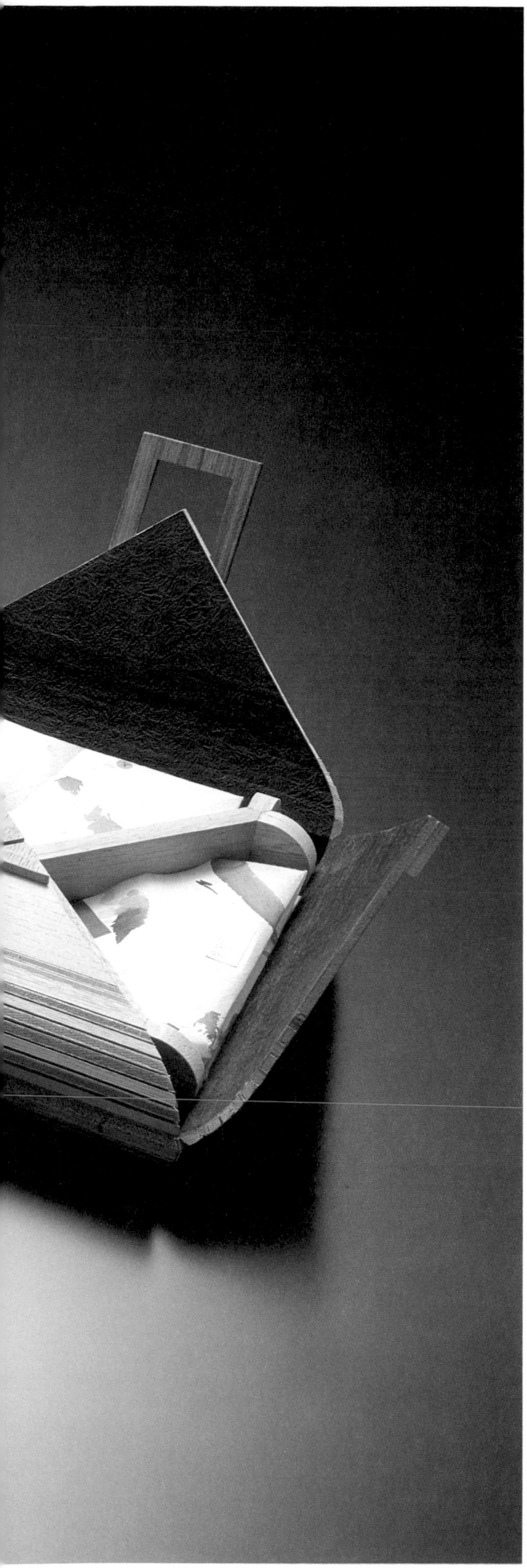

新井明子

AKIKO ARAI

Short-lived Covers.

Packaging has a pathetic life. However beautifully it may be designed, packaging is destined to be thrown away.

The act of designing packaging is putting a cover on an article for a brief period until it is handed to a user. When I came across the paulownia, a beautiful material, I felt it was rather unfair that the life of packaging is so short. Not being a professional package designer, I can, free from commercial considerations, venture to exploit my experiences and feminine characteristics in designing paulownia packaging. Thus, I decided on a modern usage of paulownia, designing boxes that will not be thrown away. Every box I create is a discovery for me.

Kurzlebige Hüllen.

Eine Verpackung hat ein mitleiderregendes Leben. Wie schön auch immer sie gestaltet sein mag, ihr Los ist es, weggeworfen zu werden. Package Design bedeutet, einem Artikel für die kurze Zeitspanne, bis er in die Hände eines Verbrauchers kommt, eine Hülle zu geben. Als ich zum ersten Mal auf das Holz der Paulownie traf, ein schönes Material, fand ich es sehr bedauerlich, daß das Leben einer Verpackung so kurz sein sollte. Da ich keine professionelle Verpackungsdesignerin bin, kann ich, ohne kommerzielle Werte in Betracht ziehen zu müssen, meine Erfahrungen als Frau beim Entwerfen von Verpackungen einbringen. So habe ich mich für eine zeitgemäße Verwendung dieses Holzes entschieden, für Kästchen, die nicht weggeworfen werden. Jede Box, die ich gestalte, ist eine Entdeckung für mich selbst.

Des enveloppes éphémères.

Un emballage a une vie pitoyable. Quelle que soit la beauté d'un emballage, son sort est néanmoins d'être jeté.

Créer un emballage signifie envelopper un article pour une courte période avant qu'il n'arrive entre les mains d'un consommateur. Quand je suis tombée sur le bois de paulownia, un beau matériau, j'ai pensé qu'il était regrettable que la vie d'un emballage soit si courte. Comme je ne suis pas une experte du design d'emballage, je n'ai pas besoin de tenir compte de la valeur commerciale de mon travail et peux ainsi exprimer mes expériences de femme en créant des emballages en bois de paulownia. Ainsi, je me suis décidée pour un usage moderne du bois de paulownia et ai choisi de créer des boîtes que les consommateurs ne jetteraient pas. Chaque boîte que je crée est une découverte que je fais pour moi.

新井亮

RYO ARAI

Up-to-date Use of Paulownia.

Japanese culture is said to be a culture of wood and paper. In fact, both wood and paper are deeply associated with the life of the Japanese in various forms. The box for cakes served at a tea ceremony house appeals profoundly to Japanese aesthetic sensitivity. The beauty of a paulownia chest of drawers masterpiece is equally appealing.

It seemed too bold to tackle the long-established paulownia box, but by having some design concept appropriate to an up-to-date lifestyle, collapsible bottle racks, gift boxes and other boxes were introduced. These can be mass produced, retaining their own characteristics and uses.

Die zeitgemäße Paulownie.

Über die japanische Kultur heißt es, daß sie eine Kultur des Holzes und des Papiers sei. In der Tat spielen sowohl Holz als auch Papier eine wichtige Rolle in verschiedenen Lebensbereichen der Japaner. Die Kuchenschachtel, die beim Tee angeboten wird, spricht im höchsten Maße das Feingefühl der Japaner an. Ebenso in ihrer Schönheit die Kommode aus dem Holz der Paulownie.

Es wäre dreist, das altbewährte Kästchen angreifen zu wollen, doch mit einem neuen Design-Konzept, das einem zeitgemäßen Lebensstil entspricht, wurden andere Geschenkkästchen, zusammenklappbare Flaschengestelle usw. auf den Markt gebracht. Diese können in Serie produziert werden und verlieren dabei dennoch nicht ihre Eigentümlichkeiten und Verwendungsmöglichkeiten.

L'usage moderne du paulownia.

On dit de la culture japonaise que c'est une culture de bois et de papier. Il est vrai que le bois et le papier s'associent profondément de toutes les façons possibles à la vie des Japonais. La boîte à gâteaux que l'on sert dans les pavillons de thé fait profondément appel à la sensibilité esthétique japonaise. La beauté d'une commode en paulownia œuvrée à la perfection est également pleine de charme.

Il paraissait trop osé de vouloir s'attaquer à la boîte en paulownia, établie depuis longtemps. Mais après avoir développé une conception du design correspondant au style de vie moderne, on a pu introduire sur le marché des étagères à bouteilles pliantes, des boîtes-cadeaux ainsi que d'autres sortes de boîtes. Ce objets peuvent être produits en masse sans pour autant perdre leurs particularités et leurs possibilités d'emploi.

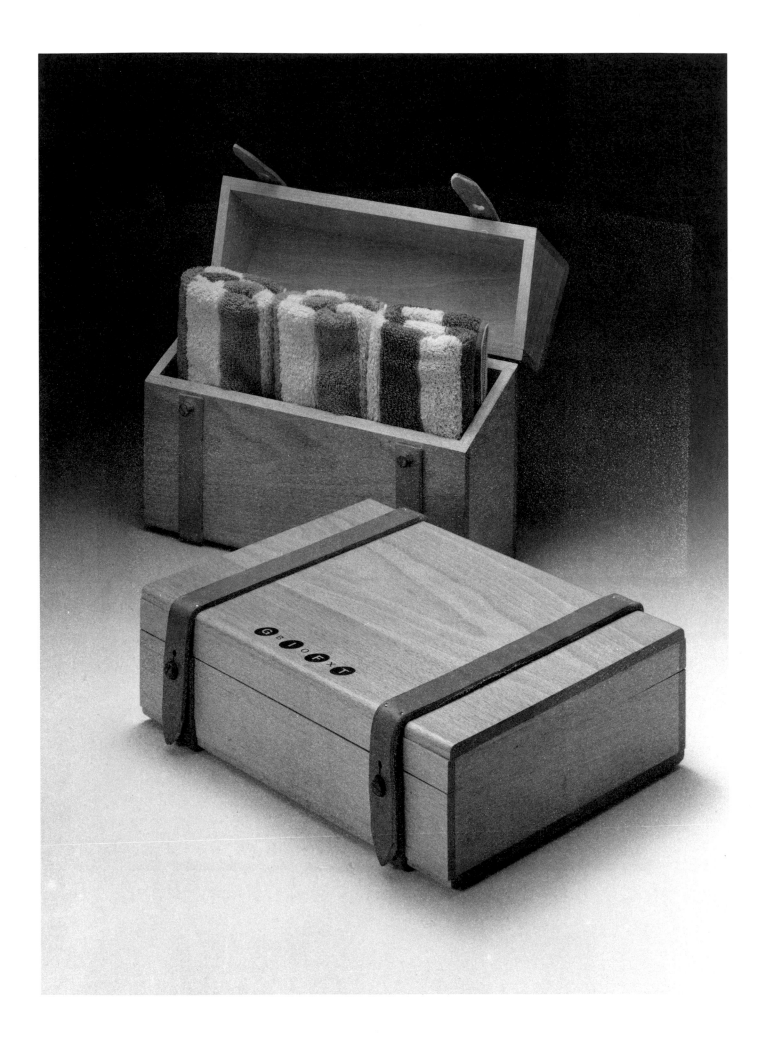

広橋桂子

KEIKO HIROHASHI

The Japanese kimono is made from a single piece of cloth with no waste. After it has served its purpose of dressing a person with beauty, it is folded into a flat square and put away in a dresser so that its shape is not destroyed. The functional beauty found in the unique style of clothing and cloth wrappers of Japan has the wisdom of the Japanese wrapped up inside of it. I have utilized this functional beauty in the creation of wrapping paper.

Der japanische Kimono besteht aus einem einzigen Stück Stoff, ohne Verschnitt. Nachdem er seinen Zweck, eine Frau mit Schönheit zu kleiden, erfüllt hat, wird er zu einem flachen Rechteck gefaltet und in die Kommode gelegt, so daß seine Form nicht zerstört wird. Die zweckbestimmte Schönheit, die wir im einzigartigen Stil der japanischen Kleidung und ihrer Hüllen vorfinden, schließt die Weisheit der Japaner in sich. Ich habe mich beim Entwerfen von Einwickelpapier von dieser funktionalen Schönheit anregen lassen.

Le kimono japonais est confectionné à partir d'un seule coupon de tissu sans gaspillage. Quand il a servi son but d'habiller une personne de beauté, on le plie en rectangle plat et le range dans une armoire pour ne pas abîmer sa forme. Cette beauté fonctionnelle que l'on rencontre au Japon dans la création de ses vêtements et de ses emballages renferme la sagesse des Japonais en soi. Je me suis inspirée de cette beauté fonctionnelle pour la création d'un papier d'emballage.

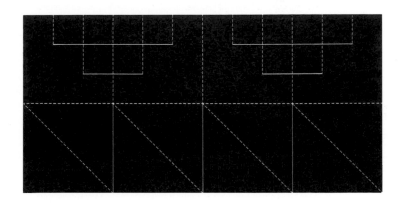

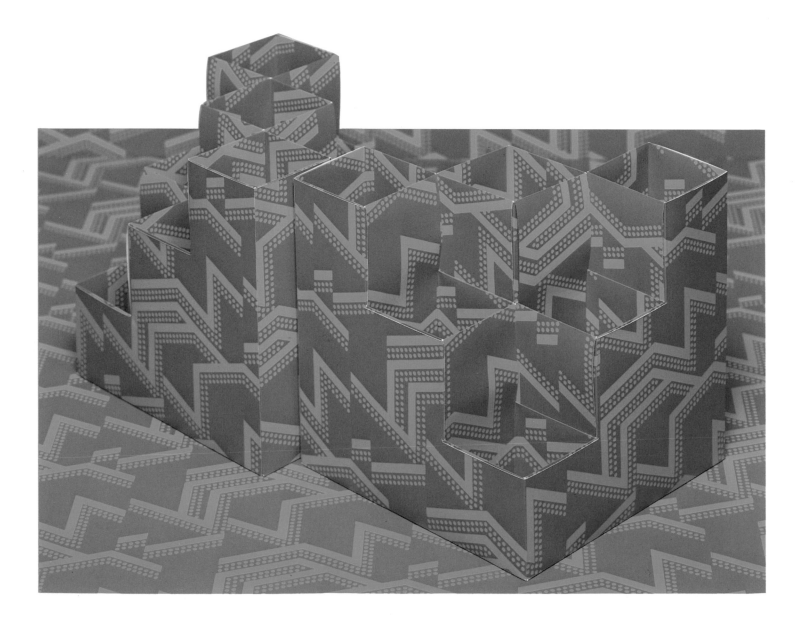

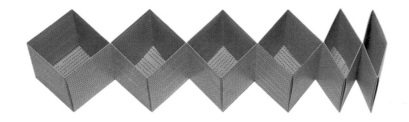

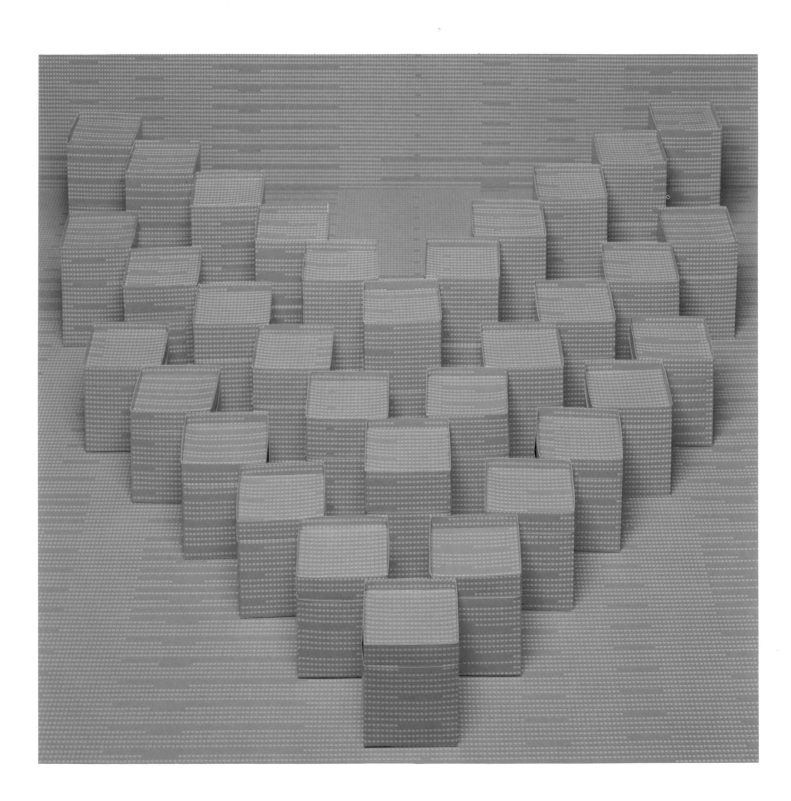

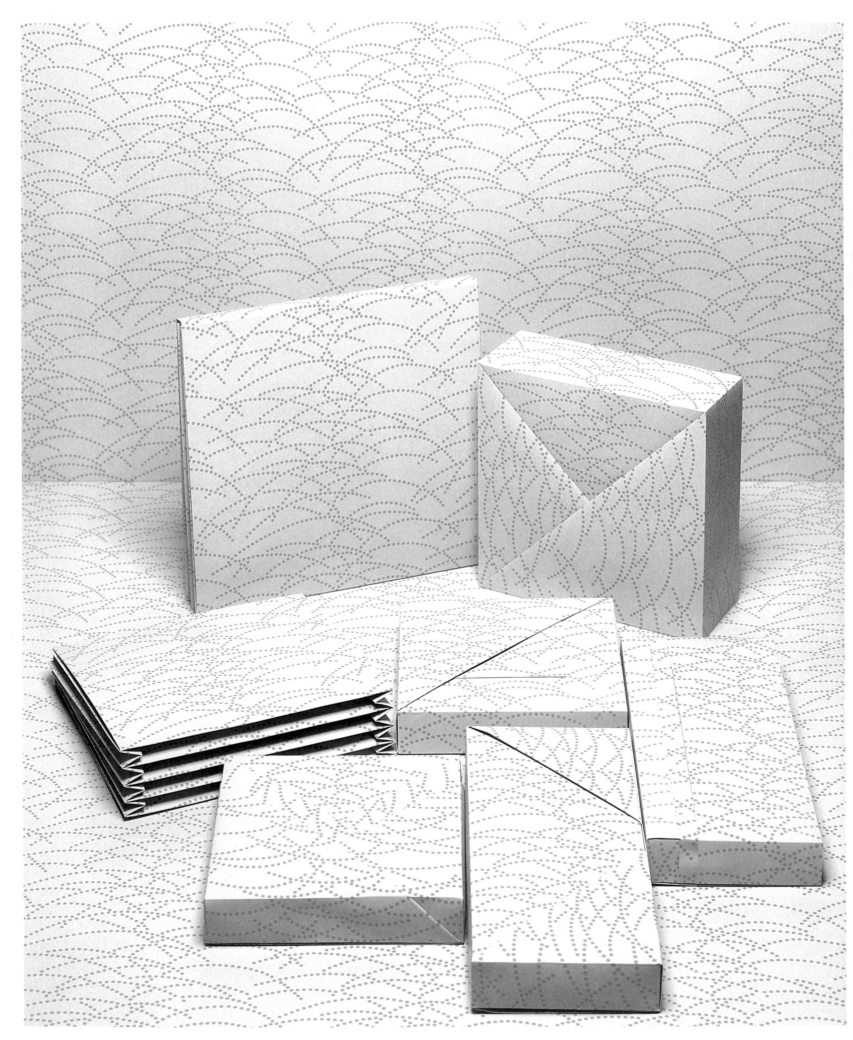

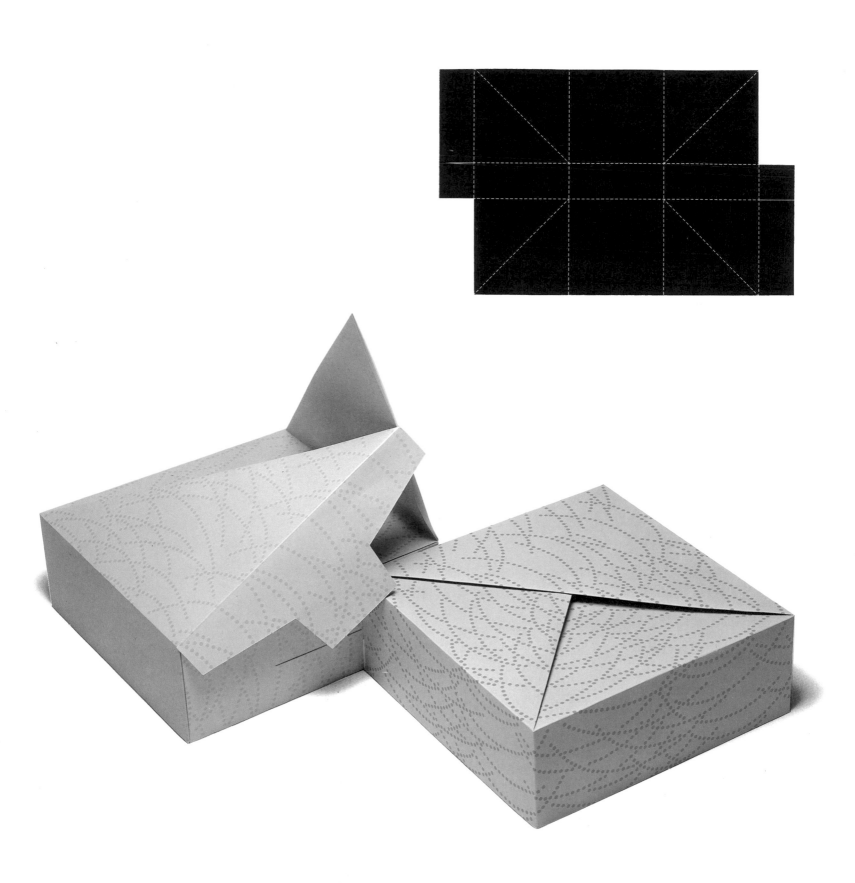

shopping bags
Tragetaschen
sacs

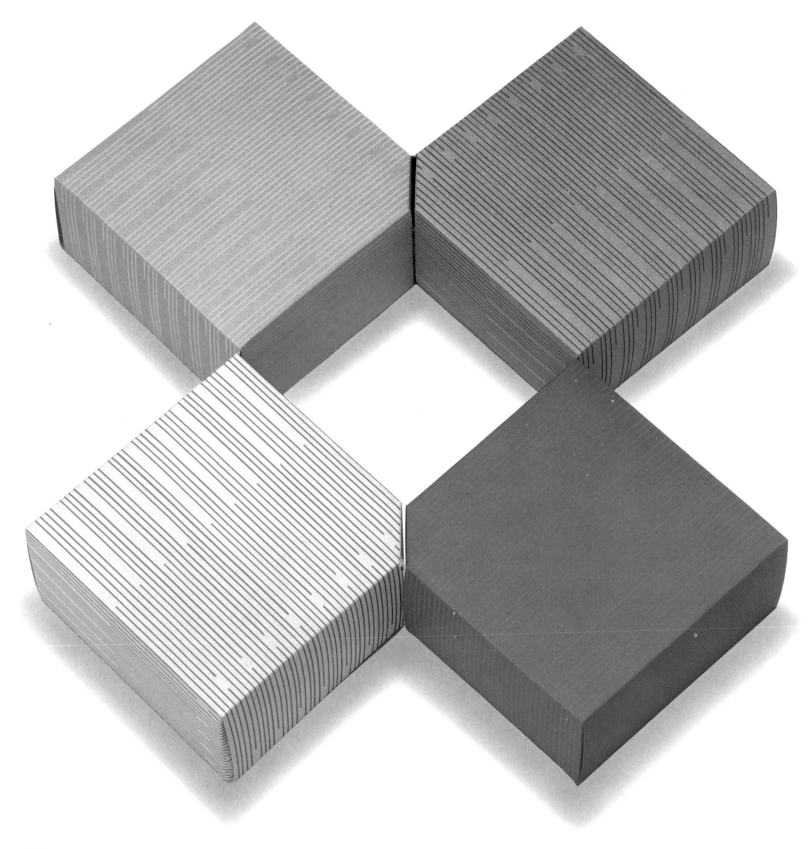

216

217

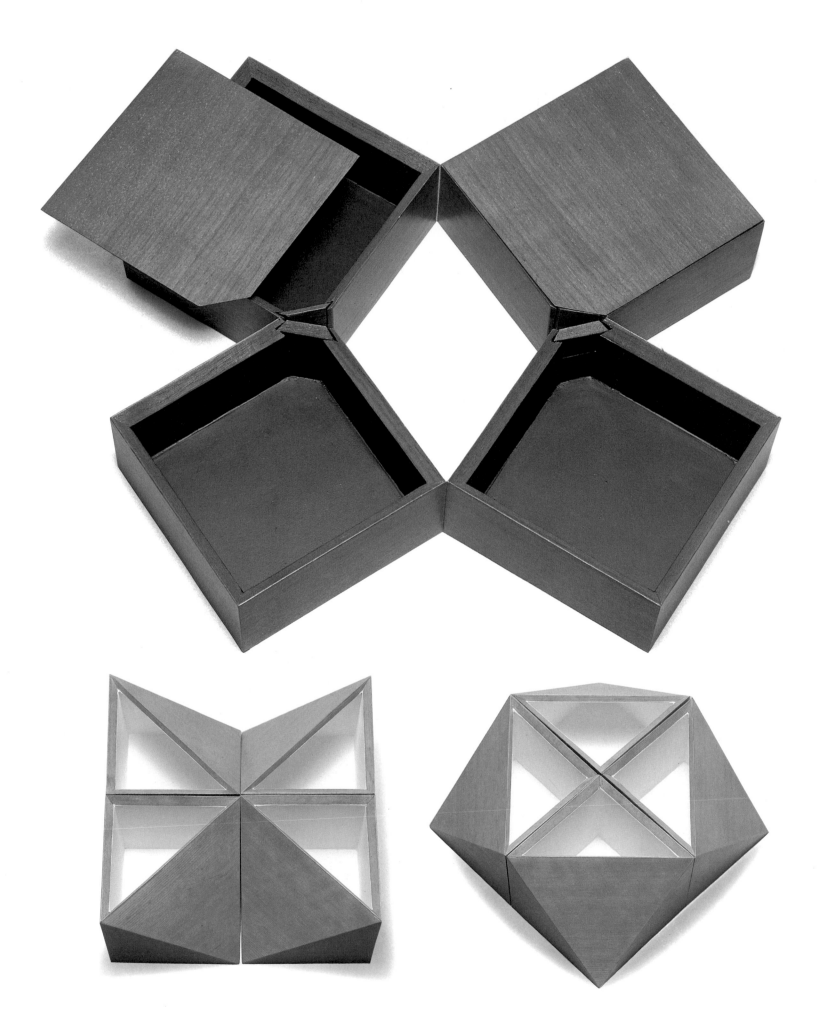

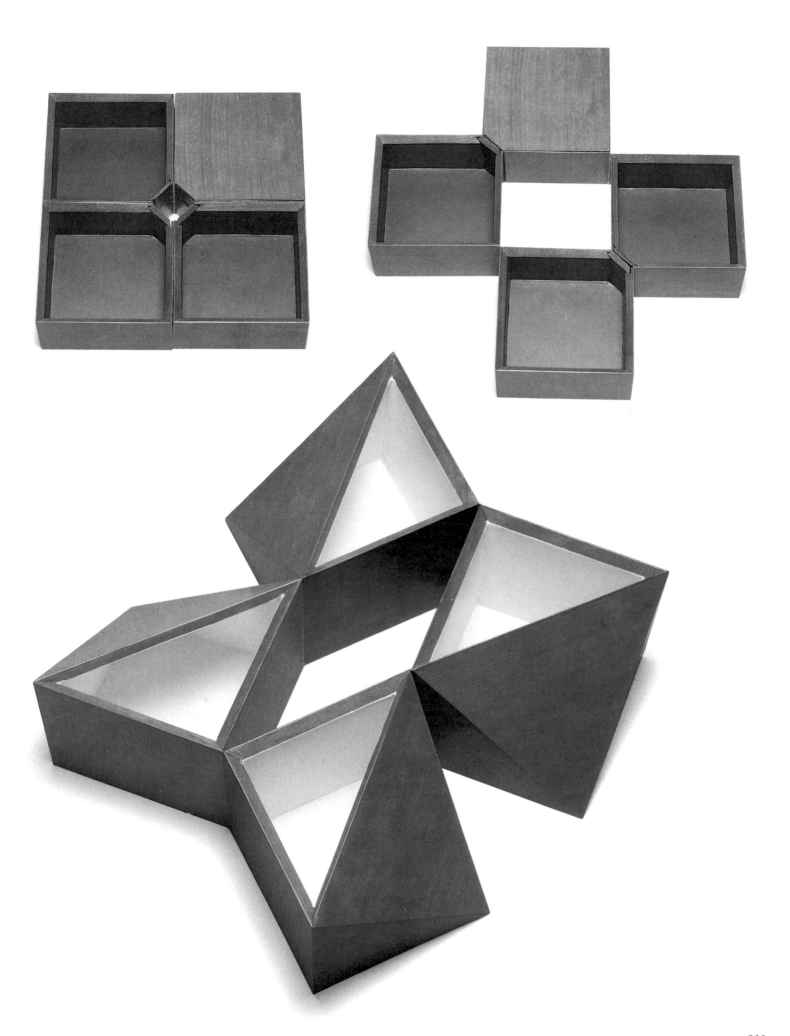

222

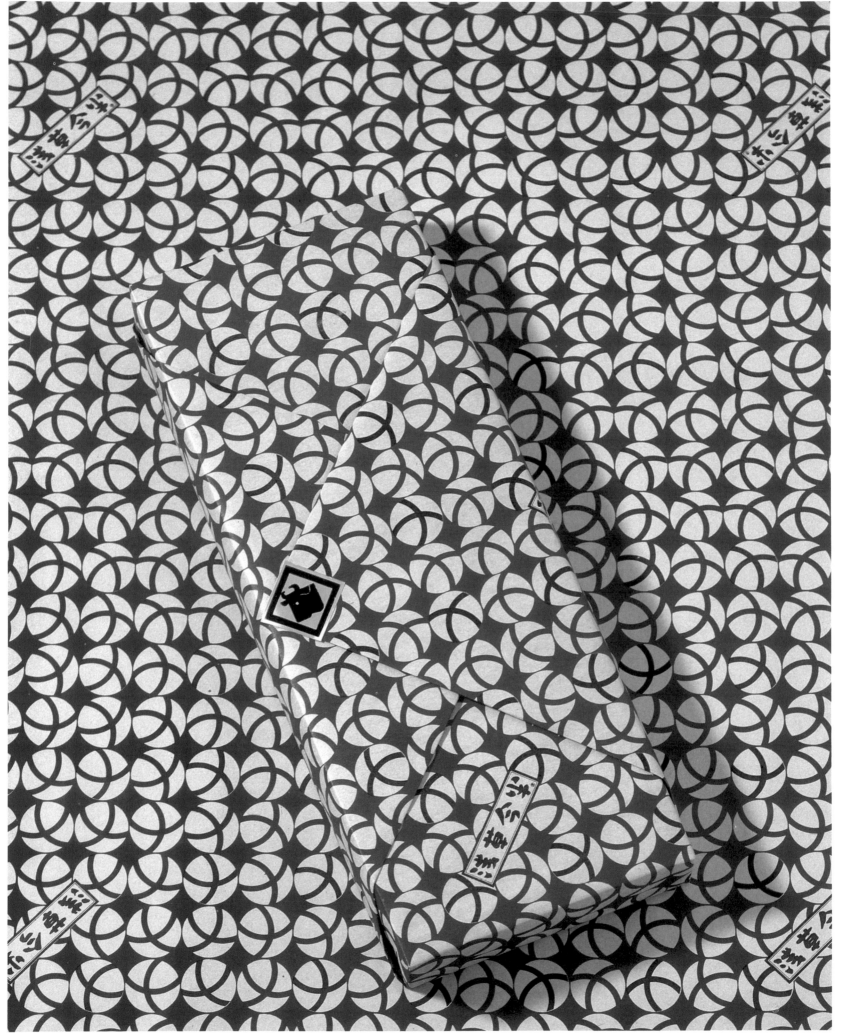

wrapping paper
Einwickelpapier
papier d'emballage

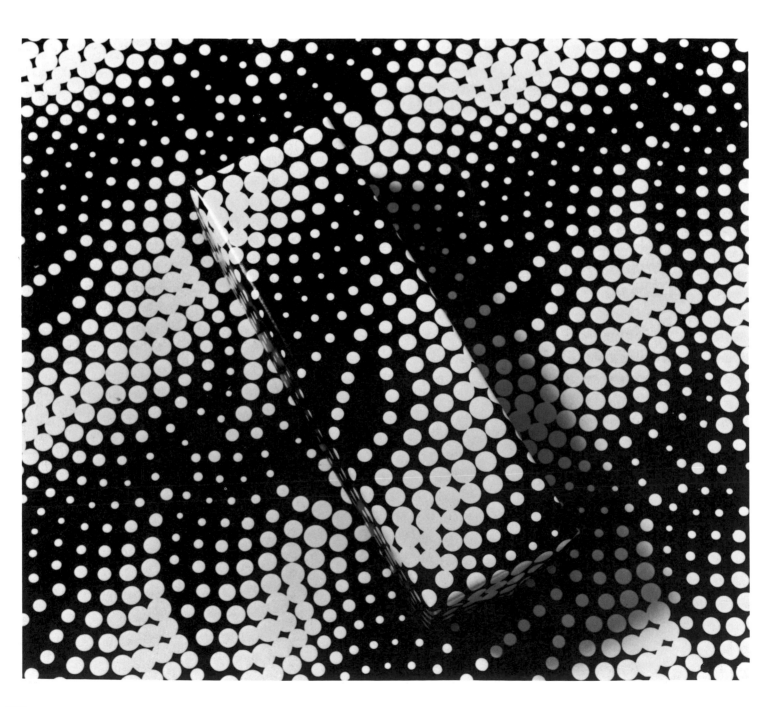

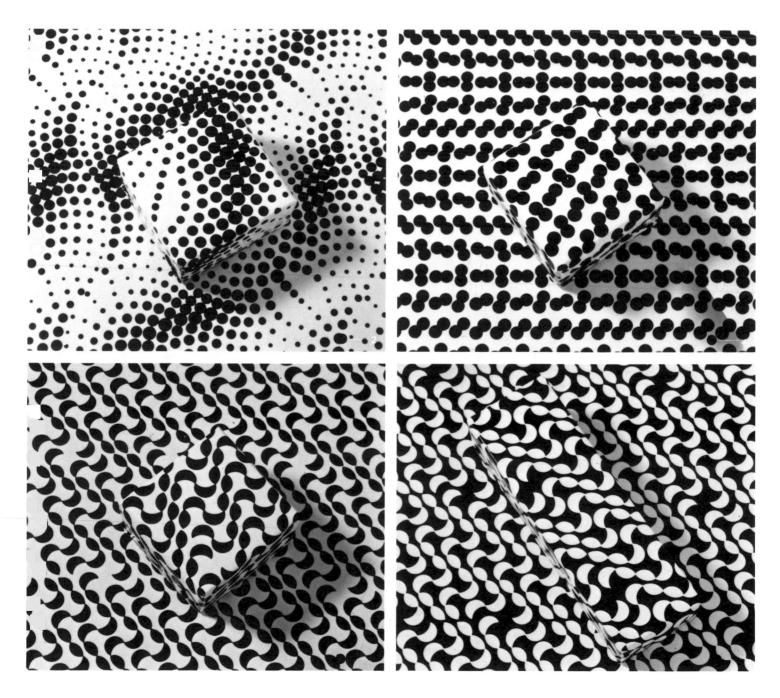

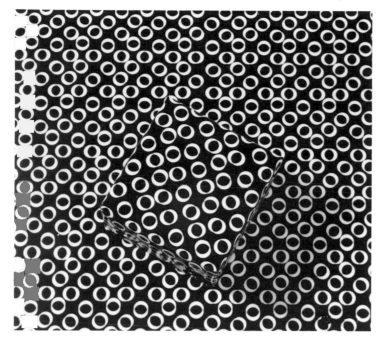
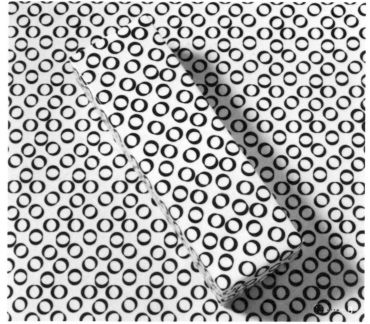

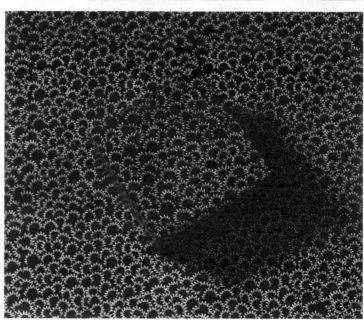

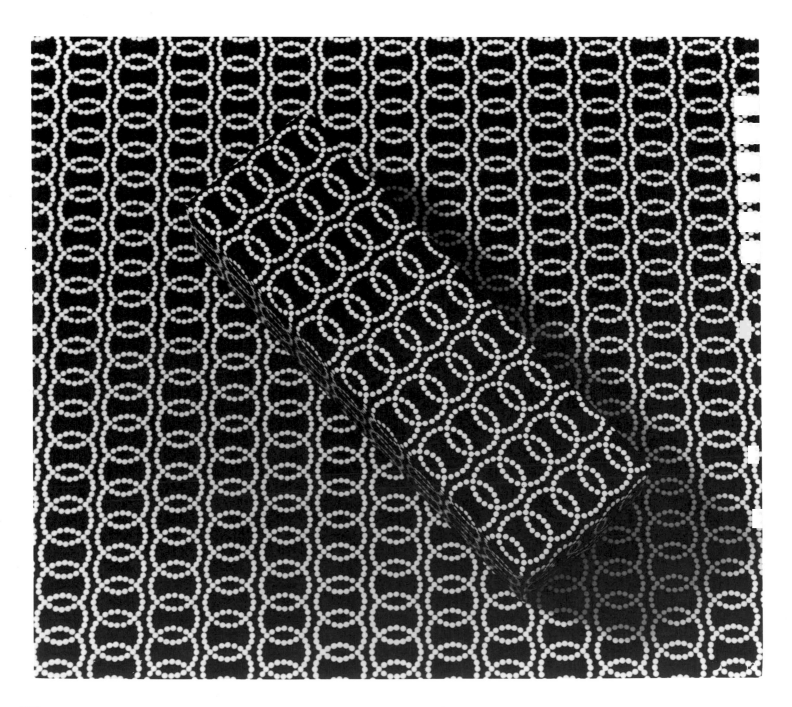

228

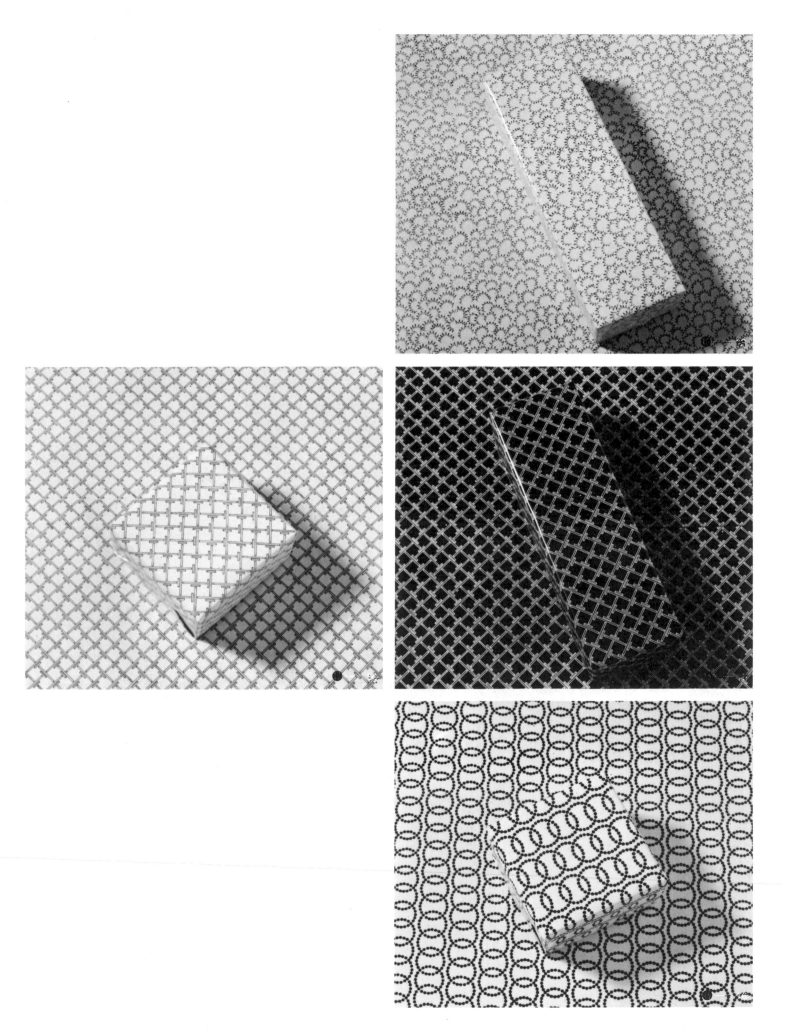

PROFILE

SHIGERU AKIZUKI

1930	Born in Tsingtao, China.	**1930**	Geboren in Tsingtau, China.	**1930**	Naît à Tsing-Tao, Chine.

1930 Born in Tsingtao, China.
1955 Graduated from Japan Advertising Art School.
Then freelance designer.
1967 Member's Award in the Fourth Japan Package Design Association Competition.
1969 Member's Award in the Sixth Japan Package Design Association Competition.
1972 Participated in the "Stop Trash Exhibition".
1973 Member's Award in the Eighth Japan Package Design Association Competition.
1976 "Prints" exhibition, Keio Dept. store.
1981 "Playing Wooden Boxes" exhibition, Hokkaido Prefectural Museum of Modern Art.
Participated in the first "4 Box-ers" exhibition, Ginza Wako Gallery, Tokyo.
1984 Participated in the second "4 Box-ers" exhibition, Ginza Wako Gallery, Tokyo.
Participated in "The 1st Wood Package Exhibition", Axis Gallery, Tokyo.
1985 Japan Package Design Award for Super Excellence and Award for Encouragement.
Featured article in Graphis no. 239 (Switzerland).
1986 Participated in "The 2nd Wood Package Exhibition", Axis Gallery, Tokyo.
Participated in "Japanese Package Design" exhibition, Purdue University, USA.
Active member of JGDA and Japan Folk Toys Society.
Lecturer, Kuwazawa Design School.

1930 Geboren in Tsingtau, China.
1955 Abschluß an der Japan Advertising Art School.
Anschließend freischaffender Designer.
1967 Preis des vierten JPDA Mitgliederwettbewerbs.
1969 Preis des sechsten JPDA Mitgliederwettbewerbs.
1972 Teilnahme an der Ausstellung „Stop Trash".
1973 Preis des achten JPDA Mitgliederwettbewerbs.
1976 Ausstellung „Prints" im Keio Warenhaus.
1981 Ausstellung „Playing Wooden Boxes", Landesmuseum für Moderne Kunst, Hokkaido.
Teilnahme an der „4 Box-ers" Ausstellung , Ginza Wako Gallery, Tokyo.
1984 Teilnahme an der zweiten „4 Box-ers" Ausstellung, Ginza Wako Gallery.
Teilnahme an „The 1st Wood Package Exhibition", Axis Gallery, Tokyo.
1985 Verleihung des Japan Package Design Award for Super Excellence sowie Förderpreis.
Feature in der schweizerischen Zeitschrift Graphis, Nr. 239.
1986 Teilnahme an „The 2nd Wood Package Exhibition", Axis Gallery, Tokyo.
Teilnahme an der Ausstellung „Japanese Package Design", Purdue University, USA.
Aktives Mitglied der JGDA and Japan Folk Toys' Society.
Vorlesungen an der Kuwazawa Schule für Design, Tokyo.

1930 Naît à Tsing-Tao, Chine.
1955 Diplômé de la Japan Advertising Art School.
S'établit ensuite à son compte.
1967 Prix du 4e concours des membres de la JPDA.
1969 Prix du 6e concours des membres de la JPDA.
1972 Participe à l'exposition «Stop Trash».
1973 Prix du 8e concours des membres de la JPDA.
1976 Exposition «Prints», grands magasins Keio.
1981 Exposition «Playing Wooden Boxes», Musée National d'Art Moderne, Hokkaido.
Participe à la 1ère exposition «4 Box-ers», Galerie Ginza Wako, Tokyo.
1984 Participe à la 2e exposition «4 Box-ers», Galerie Ginza Wako.
Participe à «The 1st Wood Package Exhibition», Galerie Axis, Tokyo.
1985 Le «Japan Package Design Award for Super Excellence» ainsi qu'une bourse de perfectionnement lui sont décernés.
Un feature à son sujet paraît dans la revue suisse Graphis, no. 239.
1986 Participe à «The 2nd Wood Package Exhibition», Galerie Axis, Tokyo.
Participe à l'exposition «Japanese Package Design», Purdue University, Etats-Unis.
Membre actif de la JPDA et de la Japan Folk Toys Society.
Donne des cours à l'Ecole de Design Kuwazawa, Tokyo.

TAKASHI KANOME

1927	Born in Hokkaido.
1950	Graduated from Tokyo Art School (now Tokyo National University of Fine Arts and Music), Oil Painting Dept.
1951	Moved to Osaka.
1966	Established the Kanome Design Office.
1968	Member of the Japan Package Design Association.
1976	Member's Award, JPDA.
1977	Silver Award at the "Japan Graphic Design New York Exhibition". Numerous awards including that of the Ministry of International Trade and Industry. Participation in many package exhibitions.
1981	Participated in "4 Box-ers" exhibition, Ginza Wako Gallery, Tokyo. Participated in "Playing Wooden Boxes" exhibition, Hokkaido Prefectural Museum of Modern Art. Asahi Newspaper Award for "Would-But-Would-Not Wood Box".
1982	Participated in the "Graphic Design Cubist Exhibition", Gallery Haku. Participated in "A Collection — An Exhibition of Clocks by 21 People".

1927	Geboren in Hokkaido.
1950	Abschluß an der Art School, Tokyo (heute die Staatliche Hochschule für Kunst und Musik, Tokyo), Fachbereich Ölmalerei.
1951	Umzug nach Osaka.
1966	Eröffnung des Kanome-Designbüros.
1968	Mitglied der JPDA.
1976	Mitgliederpreis der JPDA.
1977	Preis in Silber bei der „Japan Graphic Design New York Exhibition". Seitdem zahlreiche Auszeichnungen u. a. durch das Ministerium für Internationalen Handel und Industrie; Teilnahme an vielen Ausstellungen.
1981	Teilnahme an der Ausstellung „4 Box-ers", Ginza Wako Gallery. Teilnahme an der Ausstellung „Playing Wooden Boxes", Landesmuseum für Moderne Kunst, Hokkaido. Asahi Newspaper Award für „Would-But-Would-Not Wood Box".
1982	Teilnahme an der „Graphic Design Cubist Exhibition", Gallery Haku. Teilnahme an „A Collection — An Exhibition of Clocks by 21 People".

1927	Naît à Hokkaido.
1950	Diplômé de la Art School, Tokyo (aujourd'hui Académie Nationale des Beaux-Arts et de la Musique), Faculté de peinture à l'huile.
1951	Déménage à Osaka.
1966	Ouvre le Bureau de Design Kanome.
1968	Devient membre de la JPDA.
1976	Le Prix des Membres de la JPDA lui est décerné.
1977	Médaille d'argent à l'exposition «Japan Graphic Design New York Exhibition». A reçu depuis de nombreux prix qui lui ont été décernés entre autres par le Ministre du Commerce et de l'Industrie. Participation à diverses exposition.
1981	Participation à l'exposition «4 Box-ers Exhibition», Galerie Ginza Wako. Participation à l'expositon «Playing Wooden Boxes», organisée par le Musée National d'Art Moderne, Hokkaido. Asahi Newspaper Award pour sa «Would-But-Would-Not Wood Box».
1982	Participation aux expositions «Graphic Design Cubist Exhibition», Galerie Haku. Participation à «A Collection — An Exhibition of Clocks by 21 People».

TOSHIO SUGIMURA

1939	Born in Shizuoka.
1969	First prize, Japan Package Design Association.
1972	Ministry of International Trade and Industry's Prize (MITI), Calendar Contest. Director's Prize, Agency of Industrial Science and Technology, Packaging Exhibition.
1974	Special prizes: for Food Category, for Wrapping Paper Category, Packaging Exhibition.
1978	Established Sugi Design Institute, Inc.
1980	Silver and Bronze prizes, JPDA New York Exhibition.
1981	Director's Prize, Consumer Goods Industries Bureau, MITI, Packaging Exhibition.
1983	Prize for Encouragement, JPC Exhibition.
1984	Participated in "The 1st Wood Package Exhibition", Axis Gallery, Tokyo.
1985	Participated in the "KIBAKO" exhibition, Gallery 91, New York.
1986	Participated in "The 2nd Wood Package Exhibition", Axis Gallery, Tokyo. Since 1986 lecturer at Tokyo Metropolitan Technical High School. Active member of JPDA.

1939	Geboren in Shizuoka.
1969	Erster Preis der Japan Package Design Association.
1972	Auszeichnung im Kalenderwettbewerb des Ministeriums für Internationalen Handel und Industrie (MITI). Auszeichnung durch die Agency of Industrial Science and Technology, Ausstellung Verpackungsdesign.
1974	Sonderpreise: Verpackungsdesign, Nahrungsmitteldesign, Einwickelpapier u. a.
1978	Firmengründung Sugi Design Institute, Inc.
1980	Preise in Silber und Bronze, „Japan Package Design New York Exhibition".
1981	Auszeichnung MITI, Ausstellung Konsumgüterindustrie.
1983	Förderpreis, JPC-Ausstellung.
1984	Teilnahme an „The 1st Wood Package Exhibition", Axis Gallery, Tokyo.
1985	Teilnahme an „KIBAKO Exhibition", Gallery 91, New York.
1986	Teilnahme an „The 2nd Wood Package Exhibition", Axis Gallery, Tokyo. Lehrauftrag an der Metropolitan Technical High School, Tokyo; aktives Mitglied der Japan Package Design Association.

1939	Naît à Shizuoka.
1969	Premier Prix de la Japan Package Design Association.
1972	Mention Honorable au concours de calendriers du Ministère du Commerce et de l'Industrie Internationaux (MITI). Mention Honorable de l'Agence de la Science Industrielle et de la Technologie, Exposition de design d'emballage.
1974	Prix exceptionnels: design d'emballage, design de produits alimentaires, papier d'emballage, et autres.
1978	Fondation de l'entreprise Sugi Design Institute, Inc.
1980	Médailles d'argent et de bronze de la «Japan Package Design. New York Exhibition».
1981	Prix du MITI Exposition de l'industrie des biens de consommation.
1983	Bourse de perfectionnement décernée, Exposition JPC.
1984	Participe à «The 1st Wood Package Exhibiton», Galerie Axis, Tokyo.
1985	Participe à «KIBAKO Exhibition», Galerie 91, New York.
1986	Participe à «The 2nd Wood Package Exhibition», Galerie Axis, Tokyo. Depuis 1986 Maître de conférences au Metropolitan Technical Highschool, Tokyo; Membre actif de la Japan Package Design Association.

KATSU KIMURA

1934	Born in Ibaraki.
1956	Graduated from Japan Advertising Art School.
1964	Member's Award of the Japan Package Design Association.
1967	New York Top Packaging Award.
1969	"Padico Exhibition".
1972	Katsu Kimura Exhibition — Forms Playing Variations, Keio Dept. Store.
1974	Member's Award of the Japan Package Design Association.
1979	„Box & Cox Exhibition", Ginza Fuma Gallery.
1981	ADC Award for Katsu Kimura Package Direction. Participated in the "4 Box-ers" exhibition, Ginza Wako Gallery, Tokyo.
1982	Active member of Tokyo Art Directors' Club.

1934	Geboren in Ibaraki.
1956	Abschluß der Japan Advertising Art School.
1964	Mitgliederpreis der Japan Package Design Association.
1967	Verleihung des New York Top Packaging Award.
1969	Einzelausstellung „Padico".
1972	„Katsu Kimura Exhibition — Forms Playing Variations", Keio Warenhaus.
1974	Mitgliederpreis der JPDA.
1979	Ausstellung „Box & Cox", Ginza Fuma Gallery, Tokyo.
1981	ADC Award für Katsu Kimura Package Direction. Teilnahme an der Ausstellung „4 Box-ers", Ginza Wako Gallery.
1982	Aktives Mitglied des Tokyo Art Directors' Club.

1934	Naît à Ibaraki.
1956	Diplômé de la Japan Advertising Art School.
1964	Prix du concours des membres de la Japan Package Design Association.
1967	New York Top Packaging Award.
1969	«Padico Exhibition».
1972	«Katsu Kimura Exhibition — Forms Playing Variations», grands magasins Keio.
1974	Prix du concours des membres de la JPDA.
1979	«Box & Cox Exhibition», Galerie Ginza Fuma, Tokyo.
1981	ADC Award décerné à la Katsu Kimura Package Direction. Participation à l'exposition «4 Box-ers», Galerie Ginza Wako.
1982	Membre actif du Tokyo Art Director's Club.

U. G. SATO

1935	Born in Tokyo. Left Tokyo Gakugei University. Graduated from Kuwazawa Design School.	**1935**	Geboren in Tokyo. Studium an der Gakugei Universität, Tokyo. Abschluß an der Kuwazawa Schule für Design.	**1935**	Naît à Tokyo. Etudes à l'Université Gakulei, Tokyo. Diplômé à l'Ecole de Design Kuwazawa.
1972	"My Evolutionary Theory" exhibition, Gallery Okabe, Tokyo.	**1972**	Ausstellung „My Evolutionary Theory", Gal- lery Okabe, Tokyo.	**1972**	Exposition «My Evolutionary Theory»», Gale- rie Okabe, Tokyo.
1975	Established U. G. Sato & Design Farm.	**1975**	Gründung von „U. G. Sato & Design Farm".	**1975**	Fonde «U. G. Sato + Design Farm».
1976	"My Sense of Balance" exhibition, Fuma Gallery, Tokyo.	**1976**	Ausstellung „My Sense of Balance", Fuma Gallery, Tokyo.	**1976**	Exposition «My Sense of Balance», Galerie Fuma, Tokyo.
1977	Silver prize, Japan Graphic Design New York Exhibition. "Negative, Positive" exhibition, Fuma Gallery, Tokyo.	**1977**	Auszeichnung in Silber der „Japan Graphic Design New York Exhibition". Ausstellung „Negative, Positive", Fuma Gal- lery, Tokyo.	**1977**	Médaille d'argent du «Japan Graphic Design New York Exhibition». Exposition «Negative, Positive», Galerie Fuma, Tokyo.
1978	Japan Contemporary Prints Exhibition. Gold prize, Graphic Design Biennale, Breno, Czechoslovakia. Award, International Poster Biennale, War- saw, Poland.	**1978**	Teilnahme an der Ausstellung „Japan Con- temporary Prints Exhibition". Auszeichnung in Gold auf der Graphic Design Biennale in Brno (Brünn), CSSR. Auszeichnung auf der Internationalen Plakat Biennale in Warschau, Polen.	**1978**	Participe à l'exposition «Japan Contemporary Prints». Médaille d'or de la Biennale du Design Gra- phique, Brno, Tchécoslovaquie. Mention honorable à la Biennale Internatio- nale de l'Affiche à Varsovie, Pologne.
1979	Gold prize, Lahti Poster Biennale, Finland.	**1979**	Auszeichnung in Gold auf der Lahti Poster Biennale in Lahti, Finnland.	**1979**	Médaille d'or de la Biennale du Poster de Lahti, Finlande.
1980	"Wood Series" exhibition, Fuma Gallery, Tokyo.	**1980**	Ausstellung „Wood Series", Fuma Gallery, Tokyo.	**1980**	Exposition «Wood Series», Galerie Fuma, Tokyo.
1981	Member of the jury at Lahti Poster Bien- nale, Finland.	**1981**	Mitglied des Preisgerichts der Lahti Poster Biennale, Lahti, Finnland.	**1981**	Fait partie du jury à la Biennale du Poster de Lahti.
1982	Ipisa Graphic '82, Spain. Visual Circus Exhibition, Matsuya, Tokyo.	**1982**	Teilnahme an der Ipisa Graphic '82, Spanien.	**1982**	Participe à Ipisa Graphic '82, Espagne. Participe à «Visual Circus Exhibition», Mat- suya, Tokyo.
1983	Serigraphy exhibition, Print Gallery, Amster- dam, Netherlands.	**1983**	Teilnahme an der Ausstellung von Sieb- drucken in der Print Gallery, Amsterdam.	**1983**	Participe à l'exposition de sérigraphies à la Galerie des Estampes, Amsterdam, Hollande.
1984	"U. G. Sato's Nonsense World", IBM Kawasaki Civic Gallery. "Fence Series" exhibition, Gallery Olive, Tokyo. "The 1st Wood Package Exhibition", Axis Gallery, Tokyo.	**1984**	Ausstellung „U. G. Sato's Nonsense World", IBM Kawasaki Civic Gallery. Ausstellung „Fence Series", Gallery Olive, Tokyo. Teilnahme an der Ausstellung „The 1st Wood Package Exhibition", Axis Gallery, Tokyo.	**1984**	Exposition «U. G. Sato's Nonsense World», Galerie Civique IBM, Nagasaki. Exposition «Fence Series», Galerie Olive, Tokyo. Participe à l'exposition ‹The 1st Wood Package Exhibition», Galerie Axis, Tokyo.
1985	"U. G. Sato's Nonsense Image", Hankyu Dept. store group. "Swinging Objects" exhibition, Ikebukuro Seibu. "KIBAKO" exhibition, Gallery 91, New York. "US-Japan Peace Poster" exhibition, Hiroshima Museum und Matsuya, Tokyo. "Cag by Laser Beam" exhibition, Gallery Space 21, Tokyo.	**1985**	Ausstellung „U. G. Sato's Nonsense Image", Hankyu Warenhäuser. Ausstellung „Swinging Objects", Ikebukuro Seibu. Teilnahme an der „KIBAKO" Ausstellung, Gallery 91, New York. Teilnahme an der Ausstellung „US-Japan Peace Poster", Hiroshima Museum und Matsuya, Tokyo. Ausstellung „Cag by Laser Beam", Gallery Space 21, Tokyo.	**1985**	Exposition «U. G. Sato's Nonsense Image», grands magasins Hanyu. Exposition «Swinging Objects», Ikebukuro Seibu. Participe à l'exposition «KIBAKO», Galerie 91, New York. Participe à l'exposition «US-Japan Peace Pos- ter», Musée Hiroshima et Matsuya, Tokyo. Exposition «Cag by Laser Beam», Galerie Space 21, Tokyo.
1986	"The 2nd Wood Package Exhibition", Axis Gallery, Tokyo. "JAGDA Peace Poster" exhibition, Hiroshima Museum.	**1986**	Teilnahme an der Ausstellung „The 2nd Wood Package Exhibition", Axis Gallery, Tokyo. Teilnahme an der Ausstellung „JAGDA Peace Poster", Hiroshima Museum.	**1986**	Participe à l'exposition ‹The 2nd Wood Package Exhibition», Galerie Axis, Tokyo. Participe à l'exposition «JAGDA Peace Pos- ter», Musée Hiroshima.

KOZO OKADA

1934 Born in Osaka.

1953 Finished Osaka Municipal Miyakojima Technical High School.

1958 Graduated from Kyoto City University of Art. Employed by Renown Inc.

1961 Various prizes and awards (packaging design).

1965 Established Okada Design Office.

1969 Reorganized the office into OD Inc., involved in graphic design, packaging, advertising design, space design for restaurants and boutiques, brush art and video art.

1975 Various awards, Silver and Bronze for Sign Design Assn., JPDA, and Silver for "Japan Package Design New York Exhibition".

1980 Tokyo Biennale exhibition (sculpture).

1982 Ministry of International Trade and Industry's Prize, Calender Contest.

1984 Participated in "The 1st Wood Package Exhibition", Axis Gallery, Tokyo.

1985 "Form of Hospitality" exhibitions, Ginza Matsuya Dept. Stores, Ikebukuro, Shibuya; Gallery Space 21, Robinsons's Kasukabe. Participated in "KIBAKO" exhibition, Gallery 91, New York. Two Awards of Encouragement, JPDA Annual Competition.

1986 "Form of Hospitality" TV exhibition (March—June 1986). "The 2nd Wood Package Exhibition", Axis Gallery, Tokyo. Clio Award (for packaging). "Form of Early Spring" exhibition, Shibuya. "Form of Gift" exhibition, Yurakucho Seibu Dept. Store. Instructor for the development of merchandise of design excellence and for material development of hand-made paper.

1934 Geboren in Osaka.

1953 Schulabschluß am Miyakojima Polytechnikum Osaka.

1958 Abschluß an der Hochschule der Künste, Kyoto. Anstellung bei der Firma Renown Inc.

1961 Mehrere Auszeichnungen für Verpackungsdesign auf Ausstellungen.

1965 Eröffnung des Okada Designbüros.

1969 Dessen Umwandlung in die Firma OD Inc., zuständig für Graphikdesign, Verpackungsdesign, Anzeigengestaltung, Innendekoration und Ladenausstattung, Airbrush und Videokunst.

1975 Verleihung mehrerer Preise, u. a. in Silber und Bronze der Sign Design Assn., der JPDA und die Silbermedaille der „Japan Package Design New York Exhibition".

1980 Gruppenausstellung Tokyo Biennale Exhibition (Skulptur).

1982 Preis des Ministeriums für Internationalen Handel und Industrie im Kalenderwettbewerb.

1984 Teilnahme an „The 1st Wood Package Exhibition", Axis Gallery, Tokyo.

1985 Ausstellungen „Form of Hospitality" im Warenhaus Ginza Matsuya, Ikebukuro, Shibuya Seibu, in den Galerien Space 21, Robinson's Kasukabe. Teilnahme an „KIBAKO Exhibition", Gallery 91, New York. Zwei Förderpreise beim JPDA Jahreswettbewerb.

1986 „Form of Hospitality" Fernsehreihe von März bis Juni 1986. Teilnahme an „The 2nd Wood Package Exhibition", Axis Gallery, Tokyo. Verleihung des Clio Award (für Verpackung). Ausstellung „Form of Early Spring", Shibuya Warenhaus. Ausstellung „Form of Gift", Yurakucho Warenhaus. Beratertätigkeit zur Entwicklung des Warendesigns, der Verbesserung von Materialien und handgeschöpftem Papier.

1934 Naît à Osaka.

1953 Diplômé de l'Ecole Polytechnique Miyakojima, Osaka.

1958 Diplômé de l'Ecole des Beaux-Arts, Kyoto. Entre dans la maison Renown Inc.

1961 Plusiers prix lui sont décernés pour son design d'emballage lors de diverses expositions.

1965 Ouvre le Bureau de Design Okada.

1969 Transforme celui-ci en l'entreprise OD Inc., se chargeant de stylismes graphiques, designs d'emballages, de la composition d'annonces, de décorations intérieures et d'aménagements de magasins, ainsi que d'aérographies et d'art vidéo.

1975 Plusiers prix lui sont décernés, dont la médaille d'argent et la médaille de bronze de la Sign Design Association, de la JPDA. Médaille d'argent de la «Japanese Package Design. New York Exhibition».

1980 Exposition collective «Tokyo Biennale Exhibition» (sculpture).

1982 Prix du Ministère du Commerce et de l'Industrie au concours de calendriers.

1984 Participation à l'exposition «The 1st Wood Package Exhibition», Galerie Axis, Tokyo.

1985 Expositions «Form of Hospitality» aux grands magasins Ginza Matsuya, Ikebukuro Shibuya Seibu, ainsi qu'aux galeries Space 21 et Robinson's Kasukabe. Participe à «KIBAKO Exhibition», Galerie 91, New York. Deux bourses de perfectionnement lui sont décernées au concours annuel de la JPDA.

1986 «Form of Hospitality», série de télévision diffusée de mars en juin 1986. Participation à l'expositon «The 2nd Wood Package Exhibition», Galerie Axis, Tokyo. Le Clio Award (pour emballages) lui est décerné. Exposition «Form of Early Spring» aux grands magasins Shibuya. Exposition «Form of Gift» aux grand magasins Yurakucho. Conseiller pour la conception du design commercial, du perfectionnement des matériaux et du papier fait main.

AKIKO ARAI

Born in Tokyo.
Graudated from the Women's College of Fine Art, Tokyo.
Employed by Ichida Inc. as a textile designer.,
Employed by AD Center Inc. and by Taiwa Industry as a fashion director.
Established Acos Fabric House: Design of fashion, goods, interior design, products und the brand name of "Maison de Acos".
Participated in New York Apple Texpo.
Appointed as a member of Silk Product Promotion Round Table, MITI.
Licensed the brand Name "Maison de Acos" to the bed linen produced by Osaka Nishikawa and Mitsubishi Carolan.
Licensed the brand name to handkerchief design of Nakanishi Gihei Shoten.
Licensed the brand name to umbrella design of Miyajima Co., Ltd.

Geboren in Tokyo.
Absolventin des Women's College of Fine Art, Tokyo.
Textildesignerin bei Ichida, Inc.
Directrice bei AD Center, Inc. und Taiwa Industry.
Gründung von Acos Fabric House: Textil-. Modedesign, Innenausstattung, Gebrauchsgüter-Design, Markenprodukt „Maison de Acos".
Teilnahme an New York Apple Texpo.
Mitglied des „Silk Product Promotion Round Table" (MITI).
Lizenzvergabe der Markenbezeichnung „Maison de Acos" an die Bettwäsche-Hersteller Osaka Nishikawa und Mitsubishi Carolan.
Lizenzvergabe dieser Markenbezeichnung an das Taschentuch-Design von Nakanishi Gihei Shoten..
Lizenzvergabe dieser Markenbezeichnung an das Regenschirm-Design der Firma Miyajima.

Naît à Tokyo.
Diplômée du Women's College of Fine Arts, Tokyo.
Designer de textile chez Ichida, Inc.
Directrice du Centre Ade, Inc. et de Taiwa Industry.
Fonde Acos Fabric House: Design de textile, design de mode, aménagement intérieur, design d'articles utilitaires, marque de commerce «Maison De Acos».
Participation à la «New York Apple Texpo».
Membre du «Silk Product Promotion Round Table» (MITI).
Cession de licence de la marque de commerce «Maison de Acos» aux fabricants de literie MM. Osaka Nishikawa et Mitsubishi Carolan.
Cession de licence de cette marque de commerce aussi à M. Nakanishi Gihei Shoten pour son design de mouchoir.
Cession de licence de cette marque de commerce à la maison Miyajima pour son design de parapluie.

RYO ARAI

1933	Born in Tochigi.
1957	Graduated from Tokyo National University of Fine Arts and Music.
1958	Member of Japan Advertising Artists Club. Award for Encouragement, JAAC Exhibition.
1959	Employed by Desca under the guidance of Takashi Kono. Gold prize, Calendar Contest by Dai Nippon Printing Co., Ltd.
1960	Mainichi Advertising Prize.
1962	Freelance designer/illustrator for Hitachi, Seibu Dept. Store, Isuzu Motors, IBM, etc.
1975	Started etching.
1978	"Wood Block Prints" exhibition, Aoyama 5610 Gallery, Tokyo.
1979	"Wood Block Prints Grand Prix" exhibition, Nichido Gallery, Tokyo.
1980	"Wood Block Prints" exhibition, Ginza Mikimoto Gallery, Tokyo.
1982	Ministry of International Trade and Industry's Prize, Calendar Contest.
1983	Illustrated book "Flower Eating Lions".
1985	"Wood Block Prints", Tokyo Group Exhibition, Keio Dept. Store. Participated in "The 1st Wood Package Exhibition", Axis Gallery, Tokyo.
1986	Participated in "The 2nd Wood Package Exhibition", Axis Gallery, Tokyo.

1933	Geboren in Tochigi.
1957	Abschluß an der Staatlichen Hochschule für Kunst und Musik, Tokyo.
1958	Mitglied des Japan Advertising Artist Club. Förderpreis, JAAC-Ausstellung.
1959	Angestellter bei Desca unter Takashi Kono. Auszeichnung in Gold im Kalenderwettbewerb der Dai Nippon Printing Co.
1960	Mainichi Advertising-Preis.
1962	Als freiberuflicher Designer und Illustrator. Arbeiten für Hitachi, Seibu Warenhaus, Isuzu Motors, IBM u. a.
1975	Erste Radierungen.
1978	Einzelausstellung „Wood Block Prints", Aoyama 5610 Gallery, Tokyo.
1979	Gruppenausstellung „Wood Block Prints Grand Prix", Nichido Gallery, Tokyo.
1980	Einzelausstellung „Wood Block Prints", Ginza Mikimoto Gallery, Tokyo.
1982	Preis des Ministeriums für Internationalen Handel und Industrie im Kalenderwettbewerb.
1983	Illustrationen zu dem Buch „Flower Eating Lions".
1985	Gruppenausstellung „Wood Block Prints", Keio Warenhaus, Tokyo. Teilnahme an „The 1st Wood Package Exhibition", Axis Gallery, Tokyo.
1986	Teilnahme an „The 2nd Wood Package Exhibition", Axis Gallery, Tokyo.

1933	Naît à Tochigi.
1957	Diplômé de l'Académie Nationale des Beaux-Arts et de la Musique, Tokyo.
1958	Devient membre du Japan Advertising Artist Club. Bourse de perfectiohnement décernée lors de l'exposition du JAAC.
1959	Devient employé chez Desca sous M. Takashi Kono. Médaille d'or au concours de calendriers de l'imprimerie Dai Nippon.
1960	Prix de Publicité Mainichi.
1962	S'établit à son compte: ouvrages entre autres pour les grands magasins Seibu, ainsi que pour les maisons Hitachi, Isuzu Motors, IBM.
1975	Premières gravures.
1978	Exposition individuelle «Wood Block Prints», Galerie Aoyama 5610, Tokyo.
1979	Exposition collective «Wood Block Prints Grand Prix», Galerie Nichido, Tokyo.
1980	Exposition individuelle «Wood Block Prints», Galerie Ginza Mikimoto, Tokyo.
1982	Prix du Ministère du Commerce et de l'Industrie au concours de calendrier.
1983	Illustrations du livre intitulé «Flower Eating Lions».
1985	Exposition collective «Wood Block Prints» aux grands magasins Keio, Tokyo. Participe à «The 1st Wood Package Exhibition», Galerie Axis, Tokyo.
1986	Participe à «The 2nd Wood Package Exhibition», Galerie Axis, Tokyo.

KEIKO HIROHASHI

1931	Born in Tokyo.
1954	Graduated from Tokyo National University of Fine Arts and Music, Fine Arts Dept., Design Section. Employed by Morinaga Confectionery Company, merchandise planning section.
1962	Established Hirohashi Design Bureau.
1965	Member's Award of the JPDA Competition.
1966	Lecturer at Tokyo National University of Fine Arts and Music.
1977	"One Day One Show", Tokyo Designers' Space.
1978	Member of Design Research Unit of Tamagawa University Design Research Center.
1981	Participated in "4 Box-ers Exhibition", Ginza Wako Gallery. "Playing Wooden Boxes" Exhibition, Hokkaido Prefectural Museum of Modern Art.
1984	Participated in "The 1st Wood Package Exhibition", Axis Gallery, Tokyo. The 2nd "4 Box-ers Exhibition", Ginza Wako Gallery.
1986	Participated in "Asahi Contemporary Crafts Exhibition '86". Participated in "The 2nd Wood Package Exhibition", Axis Gallery, Tokyo.

1931	Geboren in Tokyo.
1954	Abschluß an der Staatlichen Hochschule für Kunst und Musik, Abteilung Bildende Kunst/Design, Tokyo. Danach angestellt bei dem Süßwarenhersteller Morinaga als Produktgestalterin.
1962	Eröffnung des Hirohashi Designbüros.
1965	Mitgliederpreis des JPDA Mitgliederwettbewerbs.
1966	Vorlesungen an der Staatlichen Hochschule für Kunst und Musik, Tokyo.
1977	Ausstellung „One Day One Show", Tokyo Designers' Space.
1978	Mitglied der Arbeitsgemeinschaft Designentwicklung am Designforschungszentrum der Universität Tamagawa.
1981	Teilnahme an der Ausstellung „4 Box-ers", Ginza Wako Gallery. Teilnahme an der Ausstellung „Playing Wooden Boxes", Landesmuseum für Moderne Kunst, Hokkaido.
1984	Teilnahme an der Ausstellung „The 1st Wood Package Exhibition", Axis Gallery, Tokyo. Teilnahme an der Ausstellung „The 2nd 4-Box-ers", Ginza Wako Gallery.
1986	Teilnahme an der Ausstellung „Asahi Contemporary Crafts Exhibition '86". Teilnahme an der Ausstellung „The 2nd Wood Package Exhibition", Axis Gallery, Tokyo.

1931	Naît à Tokyo.
1954	Diplômée de l'Académie Nationale des Beaux-Arts et de la Musique, section beaux-arts/design. Ensuite créatrice de présentation des produits du confiseur Morinaga.
1962	Ouvre son propre bureau de design.
1965	Prix au concours des membres de la JPDA.
1966	Devient maître de conférence à l'Académie Nationale des Beaux-Arts et de la Musique, Tokyo.
1977	Exposition «One Day One Show», Tokyo Designer's Space.
1978	Devient membre de l'équipe exécutive au Centre de Recherche du Design de l'Université Tamagawa.
1981	Participe à l'exposition «4 Box-ers», Galerie Ginza Wako. Participe à l'exposition «Playing Wooden Boxes», Musée National d'Art Moderne, Hokkaido.
1984	Participe à l'exposition ‹The 1st Wood Package Exhibition», Galerie Axis, Tokyo. Participe à l'exposition ‹The 2nd 4 Box-ers», Galerie Ginza Wako.
1986	Participe à l'exposition «Asahi Contemporary Crafts Exhibition '86». Participe à l'exposition ‹The 2nd Wood Package Exhibition», Galerie Axis, Tokyo.